A Stranger in Paris

A STRANGER IN PARIS

Germany's Role in Republican France, 1870–1940

Allan Mitchell

Berghahn Books

NEW YORK • OXFORD

First published in 2006 by
Berghahn Books

www.berghahnbooks.com
©2006 Allan Mitchell

Library of Congress Cataloging-in-Publication Data

Mitchell, Allan, 1933-
    A stranger in Paris: Germany's role in republican France, 1870-1940 / Allan Mitchell.
    p. cm.
    Includes bibliographical references and index.
    ISBN 1-84545-125-2 (pbk.)
    1. France--Foreign relations--Germany. 2. Germany--Foreign relations--France. 3.
France--Foreign relations--1870-1940. 4. Germany--Foreign relations--1871- 5.
France--History--Third Republic, 1870-1940. 6. France--Politics and
government--1870-1940. I. Title.

    DC59.8.G3M57 2005
    327.4304409'034--dc22

                                                                    2005057005

British Library Cataloguing in Publication Data

A catalogue record for this book is available from the British Library

Printed in the United States on acid-free paper

ISBN 1-84545-125-2 paperback

CONTENTS

PREFACE

*T*his book represents an attempt to relate, as concisely as possible, a history of the French Third Republic. As its subtitle indicates, particular attention is devoted here to the special relationship between France and Germany in the years between the wars of 1870 and 1940. This emphasis appears to me to be not only useful as an organizing principle but essential for our understanding. In an important sense, as I have elsewhere argued at length with copious footnotes to match, the national history of France ended in the late nineteenth century with the Franco-Prussian War. Thereafter, the experience of the French people was so intimately and inseparably related to that of their closest neighbor that a bilateral perspective becomes unavoidable. For all the contrasts between them, France and Germany together henceforth constituted the heartland of Europe. To be sure, other European nations, not to mention the United States or the French colonies, continued to play a certain part. But none was remotely so influential as Germany in determining the fate of republican France.

The centrality of the German question to French affairs is hardly a novel idea. In fact, dozens of authors have remarked on it. But they generally relegate this notion to the sideline of their concerns, or else they toss it off as self-evident. I have attempted to read and digest this vast historical literature and to incorporate it into my scheme of things. In doing so, however, I have tried to keep my lens sharply focused on this one main problem—without, at the same time, reducing the analysis to a simplistic formula. Although the facts rarely speak for themselves, in my opinion they do add up to a convincing case that conforms to the evidence.

After some experimentation with various outlines, I settled on a table of contents that contains ten thematic chapters. Consecutive narratives of the Third Republic already abound, and many episodes referred to in these pages have been frequently treated in exhaustive detail (a full bibliography of the Dreyfus Affair alone would doubtless fill up a volume of this size). My intention has been to present a fairly complete overview within a compact space, a picture that emerges more clearly as each interlocking piece is set into place, much like a jigsaw puzzle. If such a procedure does not quite qualify as a methodology, it should at least afford the reader a coherent approach to the course and character of republican France. Without the unifying theme of Germany's role in acting upon and within the Republic, this story would only become a much more random tale of successive events.

Regarding this arrangement, one caveat must be anticipated and allowed: not every piece of the puzzle necessarily has the same size or weight. No argument is made here, for example, that the movement for women's rights in France was heavily influenced by that development in Germany. If anything, it is plausible that German females were even more attached to *Kinder, Küche, Kirche* than their French counterparts. Yet it was they who gained the suffrage sooner than women in France, thereby setting an obvious and attainable goal that was finally to be realized after 1945 at the outset of the Fourth Republic. However one evaluates that achievement, it is surely an indispensable part of any modern European history, a comparative topic just as essential to the whole as, say, economic, diplomatic, or military affairs. All are best seen in a Franco-German or western European context insofar as permitted by the state of research and the amount of available evidence. After 1870, to repeat, an autonomous national history of France is no longer feasible.

Chapter One

AN UNSTABLE PAST

*F*rance's long and twisting road to a republican form of state has fascinated and sustained generations of historians. A complete bibliography of that topic, even under a fairly narrow definition of it, would surely contain several thousand titles. From our current perspective in the early twenty-first century, republicanism may seem to be an eminently suitable mode of government for the French people, the normal reflex of a talented, complex, and sometimes contentious society. But the record shows that the French nation had many miles to run before it settled on a republican solution as the best possible arrangement of public administration. Indeed, after 1870 the lingering aspiration of monarchical and imperial pretenders died hard, and only gradually did the institutions and symbols of a republican ethos in France come to be accepted as permanent.

The periodization of modern French history presents a conundrum that is unlikely ever to produce total agreement. As every browser of a well-stocked library knows, each table of contents in those many volumes at hand appears to be based on a different premise about content and chronology. At which point do we begin and end, and what do we put where? Relevant in that regard is the now fashionable hypothesis of "the long nineteenth century," according to which one must begin at least as early as Napoleon Bonaparte to define the outer limits of an epoch that lasted until the Great War of 1914. It is a tempting proposition, but there are important reasons to reject it. An appropriate start is to do so.

When the court painter Jacques Louis David conceived a portrait (in several versions) of Bonaparte after his splendid self-coronation in the cathedral of Notre Dame in December 1804, he had the new emperor standing stiffly in front of a desk on which a candle burned low, presumably after a long session of work in the wee hours of dawn. Most conspicuous among the props on display were under the table a volume of *Plutarch's Lives,* on the table a copy of the Napoleonic Code, and across the chair a sword. The first was an obvious allusion to Bonaparte's recent acquisition of his imperial status; the second, to his role as a lawgiver and administrator; and the third, to his prowess as a warlord. These are the fundamental criteria by which to judge his reign.

If the spectacle in Paris (also beautifully portrayed by David) marked the formality of Napoleon's elevation to the French throne, his official role as the nation's leading citizen had already been established long before. One need only refer to the constitution of 1799, which appointed him First Consul of the land and awarded him an extraordinary sway over virtually every aspect of the French state. We do not ordinarily turn to the text of a constitution for amusement, but the unintended humor of that turgid document is hard to miss. The First Consul, for instance, is duly instructed to consult on all matters of government with the Second and Third Consuls—after which the opinion of the First Consul alone shall suffice. Autocracy by any name smells just as sweet, and it was above all this conspicuous trait, merely ratified by the passage from Republic to Empire, that Bonaparte shared with his monarchical predecessors. Thus the French Revolution ended where it began with regal pretentions to absolutism. In that respect, unquestionably, Napoleon's despotic rule was a relapse.

To this conclusion an objection might be raised that the Revolution nonetheless lived on in that second symbol on the emperor's desk, the Code, which guaranteed the equality of all French citizens (except women and workers, that is) before the law. This lofty enlightened principle undoubtedly represented a significant ideological advance over the segmented and outrageously class-biased court system of the Old Regime. But awkwardly we must ask who actually controlled the appointment of judges to administer justice within this legal structure—to which the correct answer is unambiguously the emperor himself. In fact, his supreme right to appoint and dismiss judges at will had already been fixed in that constitution of 1799 and did not require the award of a caesar's laurel five years later. If one inquires about the most enduring legacy of Napoleonic rule, it was not judicial reform but administrative reorganization. The real jewel in Bonaparte's crown was the prefectoral system, an instrument of bureaucratic centralization that gave him an incomparable personal authority throughout France that his royal antecedents, in their day, could only dream of. In that respect, too, the French Revolution brought the aspirations of eighteenth-century monarchy to fruition.

Finally, the sword. A soldier of fortune, Napoleon rose out of the rank confusion and patriotic enthusiasm of the Revolution. He was therefore able to mobilize the French nation militarily as no monarch before him. And, indisputably, his exploits far exceeded in their European dimension even those of Louis XIV. Yet the manner of warfare conducted by him and his opponents between 1789 and 1815 was altogether typical of the eighteenth century, not of the nineteenth. To put this proposition quite simply, Napoleon and Wellington were the last major military commanders whose troop deployment and logistical support did not significantly depend on railroads. Nor did Blücher arrive at Waterloo by train. The realization that the movement of men and material under their direction was entirely by foot or horse-drawn carriage makes their accomplishments all the more astonishing, but it does not make them more modern.

These preliminary observations throw a labeling of "the long nineteenth century" into serious question. Some estimable scholars have defended that periodization to justify the inclusion of the Napoleonic Empire, and perhaps even the Revolution before it, in their analysis of an era that began, they say, in 1789 or about 1800 and lasted until 1914. Such a concept leans heavily on a tautology, however, because every epoch is necessarily a transition from one time to the next. By the three standards sketched above, it is clearly deceptive to detach revolutionary and Bonapartist France from the century in which their roots were so deeply embedded. There would be something patently absurd about dressing up Danton, Robespierre, and Saint-Just as representative nineteenth-century politicians. Besides, the very mention of these names raises another nagging problem of interpretation. What did they actually accomplish? The weight of recent historical scholarship appears to undercut a thesis that the Revolution brought an immense social upheaval. Essentially, it meant political destabilization rather than social transformation. Landholding patterns were not summarily changed, nor class distinctions suddenly abolished. What was placed into question, rather, was absolutism as a form of governance, for which Napoleon offered a last hurrah. In reality, if so, it was the eighteenth century that was long, not the nineteenth, because the French had to await Bonaparte's final defeat and exile before absolutist rule was forever banished. The nineteenth century actually did begin at Waterloo, or perhaps already near Moscow. For France, it was thereafter to be a new age of more democratic political manners, of gradual social evolution, of erratic economic expansion, of swifter warfare by rail, and of national redefinition.

Following the long eighteenth century, such innovations did not come easily, as the rapid succession of regimes after 1815 testified: from Empire to Bourbon Restoration (1815); to an Orleanist constitutional monarchy (1830); to a brief second republican experiment (1848); and then back again to a Bonapartist dynasty (1851) that collapsed lamentably in the war of 1870. Hence, French citizens born, say, in 1814 could have lived out their lives by the late century under six distinctly different configurations of government. For our purposes, the history of France during this entire agitated period from 1815 to 1870 may be identified by three predominant characteristics: the restless search for an appropriate political form; the precarious balance between Paris and the provinces; and the notable lack of a German presence in the nation's primary concerns. We need to take a look at each.

It was Albert Camus who most succinctly framed the basic dilemma of postrevolutionary France by observing that the regicide of

4

1793 was also a deicide. How was the nation, in other words, to regain its equilibrium without any resort to the principle of divine right? Thereafter the French polity was convulsed again and again by attempts to achieve a stable alternative to God-given monarchy, one that would somehow reconcile a powerful authority of the state with the constitutional rights of its citizens. But, before 1870, there was only manifest instability. The result was not merely a series of regime changes, cabinet turnovers, or replacements of one ruling figure with another. Instead, entirely different systems of government came and went with disconcerting speed.

Least promising, no doubt, was the Restoration monarchy with its unsubtle hints of a return to the status quo ante. The famous Charter of 1815 made little pretense, and less progress, in advancing democratic prerogatives to the people. There was no real ambiguity about the allegiance of the prime minister to the monarch rather than to the parliament. The insurrection of 1830—more nearly a coup d'état than a revolution—promised a better day, but that appearance proved to be a sham. King Louis-Philippe's bourgeois attire did not hide his autocratic inclinations. Manhood suffrage under the July monarchy remained strictly limited, the parliament was stacked, and the premier François Guizot saw to it that reform measures stalled. The ugly events of 1848 consequently ensued, in the wake of which the frightened populace sought an alternative authority by electing Louis Bonaparte as their president. They got more than they bargained for when Napoleon III emerged from this pseudo-republican cocoon before his hypothetically unrenewable four-year mandate expired. In many respects, notably including Baron Haussmann's rebuilding of Paris, the Bonapartist imperial regime was the most laudable of all these political incarnations, until the upstart emperor's folly and foreign adventure brought it all to grief in the inglorious debacle of 1870.

What these successive failures had in common was an inability to provide France with an adequate father figure to replace those who had reigned in the eighteenth century from Louis XIV to Napoleon. The pretenders lacked, in a word, legitimacy. What had been shattered in the Great Revolution and then briefly resuscitated by the first Bonaparte was never convincingly replaced. Such repeated frustration, compounded in the end by a crushing military defeat, cleared the way for the truly republican form of state that was to follow.

A second essential factor that marked the time before 1870 was the unsettled relationship between the French capital and the countryside. As administrative units, the provinces were no more. However else they differed, all revolutionaries of the late eighteenth century could agree on a need to curtail the authority of the provincial aristocracy. Therefore, the fabled names of Brittany, Normandy, Anjou, Burgundy, Auvergne, and the rest would have to go. They might remain on many maps and also certainly in the hearts of millions of French citizens, but they completely lost their political clout as a result of the Revolution.

The vacated place of the provinces was taken after 1790 by eighty-some French departments, in what must surely be counted as the most drastic redistricting in history. The implications were enormous. For one thing, as we saw, each department received a chief administrative officer, the prefect, the central government's man who was charged with implementing policies of the regime in Paris. At the same time, however, provincial elites were regrouping and a new term was coined, the notables, to designate an amalgam of upper-class dignitaries who would also have their say in government, especially as they were prominently represented both in local political offices and in the national parliament. This inherent clash between the forces of centralism and provincialism would persist, without satisfactory resolution, throughout the stretch from 1815 to 1870, providing a structural rationale for the recurrent dislocation and occasional violence of that era.

The third characteristic, well known and yet often neglected, is of special note here. In contrast to later years, Germany was all but absent in the foreign and internal affairs of France before 1870. The most compelling explanation is obvious: no united Teutonic neighbor stood on French borders. Napoleon's administrative and military efforts had left a patchwork of more than thirty independent states, along with a weakened Habsburg monarchy in the background. At the most, Germany was a cultural concept, a disorganized quarrelsome *Bund* of disparate regimes, and a distant object of French diplomacy.

Accordingly, the events that transpired in France between the military disasters of Waterloo and Sedan can be largely understood without particular reference to *"outre Rhin,"* an expression that well conveyed a French sense of vagueness about what was happening in the dark forests of central Europe. At least that was so until the late 1860s, when Napoleon III—who had been raised in Swiss exile and always spoke French with a German accent—began to test his mettle against Otto von Bismarck's Prussia. Not for the first time nor the last, irreconcilable ambitions for the Rhineland came into play, and we know the humiliating outcome for France. It was indicative that officers of the *État-Major* in Paris entered the war of 1870 with high optimism, imagining that a victorious French army would conduct a swift and successful campaign on German soil before returning to the acclamation of cheering crowds. They failed to reckon with the thoroughness of Helmuth von Moltke's planning or the rapidity of his railway convoys. Every two French soldiers were therefore met on the frontier by three German grenadiers, and the Bonapartist dynasty was quickly defeated and unseated. One era thereupon ended and another began.

An initial definition of the French Third Republic, then, can be stated in terms of what it was not. Reversing earlier trends, the fledgling state in the years after 1870 displayed none of the three main characteristics of the various regimes that had preceded it since 1815. First, the republican government became solidified and was supported by a majority of its citizenry. Second, within this innovative and enduring republican consensus a stable administrative equilibrium was established in which Paris and the provinces could reach a viable if not always harmonious relationship. Third, from its first day to the last, the Third Republic was constantly confronted in all aspects of public life with an imposing German presence in its midst. Henceforward, the most vital issue of French politics, in the largest sense, was the German question. That primary fact continued to pertain between 1870 and 1940 whether France was facing an imperial, republican, or fascist German regime. Germany was to change in appearance over time, but for France the irrepressible challenge of a formidable Teutonic neighbor remained. The stranger had come to stay.

Chapter Two

AN IMPROVISED STATE

*T*he peculiarity of the Third Republic was that it both began and ended with a devastating military defeat at the hands of Germany. That fact did not entirely define the French state between 1870 and 1940, but it did importantly affect its course and character.

In the beginning was war. As is so often the case in a conflict of armed nations, it came largely as the result of bungling and confusion—at least in France, which displayed, moreover, a massive dose of overconfidence. The key was railways. Whereas German convoys sped unimpeded to the front, French trains ferried droves of troops right into the bottleneck of the capital city, where they remained stranded for days within the ambient pandemonium. As a consequence, the French army corps found themselves outnumbered and outgunned in the border areas, enabling German forces to seize the first initiative. The French collapse at Sedan inexorably followed, and the way was open to Paris. Surrounded troops in the fortress of Metz capitulated, one of the largest mass surrenders in history. Thereafter the inevitability of defeat was never in serious doubt. The invader had his way, sweeping aside remnants of France's regular army and ill-equipped squads of hastily organized militia. An armistice was formally signed at the end of January 1871 and the first republican elections, demanded by Bismarck in order to conclude the peace,

9

were scheduled for 8 February. The big winner was Adolphe Thiers, who now functioned as head of state (soon to be president). With his foreign minister Jules Favre, Thiers conducted negotiations at Bismarck's villa in Versailles. In return for maintaining control of the fortress at Belfort, a rare symbol of French resistance, they agreed to submit to a brief German occupation of Paris and a ceremonial military spectacle in the heart of the capital. Accordingly, in the morning hours on the first day of March 1871, long columns of German soldiers (including a young officer named Paul von Hindenburg) paraded down the Champs-Élysées, the Arch of Triumph looming in the background, creating a scene almost identical with the one to be photographed there nearly seventy years later.

Although Paris was promptly evacuated, the German occupation was by no means at an end. To understand the postwar years, it is essential to recall the neglected fact that eastern France long remained under German military rule, forty-three departments in all, some of which lived under the daily surveillance of a German garrison for more than three years. That presence was felt throughout the land, even after the final withdrawal of occupation troops across the newly traced border that thereafter separated France from the annexed provinces of Alsace and Lorraine. Hence the French faced repeated "war scares" during the following two decades, a calculated attribute of Bismarck's policy of isolation and intimidation. The last notable episode of that sort occurred as late as 1887, at the time of the Boulanger crisis, when the German chancellor raised an international alarm in order to facilitate passage of increased military spending.

If the French republican leadership learned to live with such bullying, it did so at some political expense. Starting with Thiers, government officials were always vulnerable to allegations that they were toadying to German interests. The amputation of Alsace-Lorraine and the acceptance of a heavy reparations burden of five billion francs, which left the French state treasury strapped for years, were festering wounds that would not entirely heal. They help to explain the sense of betrayal and lingering dissatisfaction that erupted in the capital and several other major cities in the spring of 1871.

Seen from a military standpoint, the importance of the Paris Commune has been greatly exaggerated. The truth is that the war had already been lost at the frontier in its initial weeks. The professional French army was all but finished within days and Léon Gambetta's irregulars were no match for the efficient firepower of disciplined Prussian divisions. Paris was therefore quickly encircled and, in effect, remained helplessly trapped under siege from March to May 1871. The heroic fantasy that the Commune bravely resisted during all that time is misconceived. Moltke held the entire Île de France in a tight grip while representatives of Thiers and Bismarck meanwhile conferred in Brussels. Not until a deal between them was concluded in the Treaty of Frankfurt on 10 May was the deadlock broken. French prisoners of war and their captured *chassepôts* were thereupon returned, while trains loaded with men and munitions were again allowed to circulate. Thus strengthened and cleared for action by the German chancellor, Marshal MacMahon's troops were able to make short work of the Paris communards, whose final gesture of defiance in the cemetery of Père Lachaise was as futile as it was courageous.

The Commune, with its concluding *semaine sanglante,* nonetheless retained a robust afterlife in the mythology of the French Left, and this enduring political vitality has become its true significance. From Marx to Lenin and beyond, the message was that the valiant struggle in the streets of Paris in 1871 was the harbinger of a new society. The veracity of that assertion must be coolly measured against the reality of the Third Republic that actually ensued. In the short term, the Commune served mostly to discredit the legitimate aspirations of the French working class and thus to abet Thiers in his rigorous suppression of it during the decade of the 1870s. Thousands of ordinary Frenchmen, as well as some women, were tried, sentenced, imprisoned, executed, or exiled before an amnesty was finally declared in 1880. In the meanwhile, a middling Thierist republican form of government was founded that honored existing social arrangements and restricted any manner of radicalism. Monitored closely by Bismarck, who also exploited the bogey of the Commune for his own reactionary purposes, this troubled inauguration of a moderate public order in France would leave a deep impression on the nation from that time forward.

Shrouded by a calamitous military defeat, initially dominated by a foreign power, somewhat fortuitous in its origins, the unplanned improvisation of the Third Republic was soon to be reflected in its laws, institutions, and celebrations. By their fruits ye shall know them, the Scripture says, and the republicans proved true to their word. The new legislation notably included more liberal press laws, deregulation (for example, of bistrots and alcoholic beverages), obligatory and free public schools, and the open election of mayors by municipal councils—all departures from the authoritarian practices of previous regimes.

Despite the confused muddling of the first decade, insofar as the modalities of government were concerned, a clear pattern emerged. The lost war required a convenient scapegoat, for which Napoleon III—guilty as charged of arrogance and negligence—was the perfect candidate. It could not be surprising, therefore, that the republican presidency proved to be a relatively ineffectual office, far removed from the more imposing monarchical and imperial executives that were now discredited. Instead, the fulcrum of state authority was shifted by the constitution of 1875 to a bicameral legislature. Ever since the Great Revolution, popular assemblies had played a more or less prominent role in French affairs, but they had all been exercises in political frustration. Now in republican France the parliament both reigned and governed; and, after the 1870s, the prime minister was unambiguously its man, chosen on the basis of a multiparty system of elections with universal male suffrage. That arrangement would hold until interrupted briefly by the Vichy regime in 1940. It would thereafter be restored under the Fourth Republic and not significantly altered before the advent of General de Gaulle's Fifth Republic in 1958. In short, what was wrought in 1870 would endure for nearly a century. It must have seemed to a vast majority of the French populace that their struggle for self-definition had at last ended and that they had found their predestined form of government. The improvised state thereby became eternalized, while the assumption imperceptibly grew that France's republicanism was etched in marble, as it often was on the façade of public buildings.

That impression was strengthened through the gradual adoption of national symbols. These generally struck chords of patriotic resistance that harkened back to the Revolution. The strident melody and text of the *Marseillaise* became the national anthem. In spite of considerable opposition (by those for whom it evoked the guillotines of the Terror), 14 July was enshrined in 1880 as the national holiday. Likewise, the tricolor easily outpointed the white flag of disgruntled monarchists. And the busts of one Napoleon or another were replaced in thousands of city halls across the country by the appealing statue of an idealized and, it must be added, sexy Marianne, the allure of *la douce France* in person. All the while, unseen but omnipresent, was the accompanying republican mantra of *laïcité,* a notion that underlay all of the above. Namely, the new consensus presumed that republican France should have a secular state, thereby flaunting a principle that was bound to provoke conflict with the Roman Catholic Church, long ago established as the state religion by the Napoleonic Concordat of 1801.

Consensus is the proper term, and one does well to insist on it. The story of the Third Republic is too frequently presented as a tiresome narrative of congenital instability, a tale repeatedly marked by swift cabinet turnovers and a constant coming and going of ministers. Yet, true as that was, such commotion may be viewed paradoxically as a political manifestation of fundamental stability. In reality, except for the extremes of far Left and far Right, the republican form of state was never seriously in question after the 1870s. Precisely because everyone knew that a reshuffling of the ministerial deck was no threat to the continuity of basic republican principles, French voters and their parliamentary delegates were free to dabble at will with electoral combinations. For all the fuss, the same men came from the same parties, striking deals and moving from one ministry to another, all in service of a state for which they could imagine no suitable alternative. Throughout the existence of the Third Republic, the middle would hold.

So far as the political Left was concerned, it took fully two decades to recover strength. Persecution of the 1871 communards continued after the fall of the Thiers administration in 1873—by which time more than forty-five thousand "criminal" files had come before the courts—and a general amnesty was long delayed. Before the 1880s the quiescence of the working class was enforced by the gavel, the guard, and on occasion the guillotine. And for years afterward, to state the obvious, French *patrons* remained far better organized than their laborers. Strikes were still seldom and invariably ineffectual. The bare beginnings of a revival of French socialism coalesced around the amnesty issue. Yet it would be premature to speak of a coherent leftist political movement before the late 1880s. That development would have to await another day and the appearance of a new leadership.

Such was assuredly not the case of the Right, whence arose the main opposition before 1890 to establishing a centrist republican state. Initially that challenge came largely from ousted monarchists and Bonapartists. The former took the form of fusionism, an attempt to coordinate the efforts of Bourbon and Orleanist pretenders. This strategy foundered, however, on the rigid intransigence of the Comte de Chambord and the general ineptness of all concerned. Bonapartism fared scarcely better after the exiled Napoleon III died in January 1873 on an English operating table and his son, serving with a British expeditionary force in Africa, was killed by the Zulus in 1879. There would be no Restoration this time, not even a Hundred Days.

That verdict was hardened by a ministerial flap in 1877, known as the *seize mai* crisis, which deserves more attention than it has received. As Thiers's successor in the presidency, Marshal MacMahon's main function was to keep the door ajar for some eager royal candidate. But his abrupt dismissal of the Jules Simon cabinet forced everyone's hand and exposed the weakness of his own. Only two years after a phony but unnerving war scare in 1875, Bismarck once more waded into French politics with a threat of armed intervention if France opted for the rightist cause. It is impossible to measure accurately the impact of such imprecations, but the electorate was clearly unwilling to take chances by turning out the republicans. The hero of the day was Léon Gambetta, still renowned for his resistance to German aggression in 1870 but who now reassured Berlin—and the French public—of his peaceful intentions. Thiers's death during the ensuing electoral campaign left Gambetta as the major active founder and proponent of republicanism, and his victory over MacMahon's disunited followers assured its perpetuation. Confronted by Gambetta's taunt that he must consequently "submit or resign," MacMahon disappeared in 1879, taking the last hopes of a resuscitated royalism with him. How many small French towns, as a result, now boast a Rue Gambetta?

Bonapartism enjoyed a revival of sorts with the Boulanger affair in the late 1880s. This scurrilous episode was spurred by the Schnaebele incident, an insignificant frontier conflict (after a minor French official accidentally stepped across the border and was arrested by the Germans) that was conflated into an affront to French national honor. Presenting himself as an ardent patriot willing to defy German blustering, the former Minister of War Georges Boulanger earned the sobriquet of *"Général Revanche"* and parlayed that notoriety into victories in several parliamentary by-elections. After he had thus attracted a broad range of malcontents from both extremes of the political spectrum, so the familiar story goes, he was urged to seize the presidency: "to the Élysées," shouted crowds in the streets outside Maxim's, where Boulanger was dining one evening in Paris. All of which was a deep embarrassment to the current French regime and, as mentioned, also a welcome boost for Bismarck, who promptly made use of the matter to obtain a favorable vote in the Reichstag on raising military appropriations. Lacking the courage of others' convictions, nevertheless, Boulanger chose to withdraw and to commit suicide on the grave of his mistress.

Although the Boulanger fiasco may be judged to have had no lasting importance, other than as one more fizzled attempt to fracture the republican consensus, it does merit a few pertinent observations. In the first place, it should be noted that Boulanger was launched as a leftist officer by none other than Georges Clemenceau, that inveterate opponent of all rightists and clericals. While latter-day Bonapartists were attracted to Boulanger's candidacy, he actually had little political connection with them, apart from a staged and then widely publicized meeting with some family members in Switzerland in 1888. Yet many saw him as a Bonaparte-like figure, a man on horseback upon whom they projected their personal ambitions and overt hostility to Germany. With his abrupt self-destruction Boulanger took Bonapartism, twice buried, to its final resting place in his obscure tomb.

Thereafter, the far Right was mostly active in the form of the so-called "leagues," which were free-wheeling factions that proved in fact to be only symptomatic of a political impotence. They solely had the power to agitate. The largest and best known of these was the *Action Française,* a movement that was to remain an anomalous staple of French public life well into the interwar years. Anomalous, that is, because it was led by Charles Maurras, whose stubborn allegiance to the failed cause of monarchism was a crippling restraint. In many ways, a much more characteristic rightist personality of the postwar years was Paul Déroulède, who founded the *Ligue des patriotes* in 1882. Once a close friend of Gambetta, he later evolved to a Boulangist, a germanophobic revanchist, and eventually an anti-Dreyfusard. With like-minded of the extreme Right, he became, in short, a fierce and undiscriminating foe of the Republic, which he accused of subverting true French values and bowing all too meekly before the foreign conqueror.

These examples raise a flag of caution about focusing exclusively on the history of the Third Republic in terms of Left versus Right. One is struck by the notable frequency with which public figures changed their political affiliation and especially by the drift from one end of the spectrum to the other by men like the general Boulanger, the politician Déroulède, and also for instance the brilliant publicist Henri Rochefort. What such turncoats shared was not a fixed set of ideological principles but a flagrant French patriotism, tinged with an avowed xenophobia, that increasingly came to define the antirepublican Right. At the time of the armistice in 1871, it had been the political Left from Gambetta to the communards who wanted to fight on against the invader, whereas the Right (which dominated the first republican parliament) urged capitulation. Yet with the progressive entrenchment of republicanism, a sea change occurred. By the 1880s the Left had become conciliatory toward Germany—and thus more accepting of the loss of Alsace-Lorraine—whereas the Right now insisted on intransigence and open hostility toward the Teutons. These were fundamental attitudes that were to persist, as the much later debates over the Treaty of Versailles in 1919 would illustrate. Whatever else we may judge about the early years after 1870, then, one must conclude that a German presence hovered over French affairs and, directly or indirectly, exercised a powerful influence on the formation of republican France.

Chapter Three

A VOLUNTARIST ETHIC

*A*t any time since the Second World War—and it is true up to the present day—most observers would surely have classified France as a classic example of central planning, widespread health-care coverage, and generous public welfare legislation. That impression has been nowhere more deeply entrenched than within the French population itself, which now has every reason to worry about attempts by its government to restrict medical benefits, old-age pension plans, and other social entitlements.

It has not always been so. Throughout the nineteenth century, in fact, the opposite was true. Before 1940 republican France was above all a land of voluntarism, a trait perhaps more pronounced there than elsewhere in western Europe. Certainly, when measured by the fitting comparisons with Britain and Germany, such was the case. The intellectual roots of this deep-seated public ethic can be traced to liberalism, which in France—unlike the other comparable nation-states—did not become embodied in a single political movement but remained a pervasive factor in the way ordinary people conceived of their lives and conducted their daily business. To be liberal at the time of the Third Republic was to place emphasis on individual rights, to distrust intervention by state agencies into the private sphere, and in economic terms therefore to favor free enterprise without undue encumbrances of governmental regulation.

Probably the most telling illustration of the voluntarist ethic was a French mode of tax collection, enforced during the entire nineteenth century, called "doors and windows" (*portes et fenêtres*). The idea was simply that the state fiscal authorities should not be permitted to enter a private residence in order to estimate its value for the purpose of taxation. Rather, they should literally stand outside a dwelling and count its apertures. Only external signs of wealth—also including the number of horses and carriages owned or the servants employed—were to be considered in determining the amount owed by individuals to the state treasury. *Inspecteurs des finances* were prohibited from peering over the shoulder of a homeowner who was in the process of drafting a ledger of income and expenses. The same applied to the records of private enterprises, whose profits and losses were declared without close scrutiny by state auditors. Hence the republican parliament legislated no regular system of income assessment, and the main source of state revenue remained the property tax. A national income tax was not introduced until January 1914 and was, as we can well imagine, only very erratically enforced in the crisis and confusion that immediately followed.

Such an orientation of public manners extended also into the realm of medical practice. A single incident was altogether indicative: the response to an outbreak of smallpox (*variole*) in Paris just before and during the German siege of 1871. Reduced to its simplest terms, the situation was that the populace of the capital was not inoculated against the disease, whereas the surrounding Prussian army was. Consequently, while an epidemic ravaged the city, killing thousands, German troops remained almost entirely untouched. After the fall of Commune, however, some French prisoners of war were transferred to camps in northern Germany, where civilians had not been systematically inoculated. The swift result was the spread of smallpox there (meanwhile Bavaria, which had already enforced an obligatory vaccination program, was spared), prompting the Reichstag in 1874 to adopt legislation for mandatory vaccination throughout Germany. By 1880 the disease had virtually disappeared east of the Rhine. In 1886, a French health officer reported, France incurred fifteen thousand deaths through smallpox, all of Germany but 225. In the early Third Republic, nonetheless, the principle of obligation was still thought more suitable for an authoritarian German nation and its disciplined Teutonic citizenry than for the French. The state, it was generally assumed, did not have the prerogative to inoculate a child without a father's permission. Vaccination remained voluntary, with the result that for the next thirty years some ten thousand French men, women, and children annually died of smallpox—although physicians and politicians were aware that this severe loss of life could be avoided by following the German lead. Not until 1902 did a national smallpox vaccination program become mandatory in France.

Public health plans were drafted accordingly. Whereas Bismarck's Kaiserreich proceeded to lay the foundations of a national insurance and pension system, obligatory at first for industrial workers and later for agricultural and forestry labor as well, republican France chose voluntarism in the form of mutual aid societies. Mutualism was available only to those employees who regularly contributed to small private groups, usually comprising local clusters of like-minded religious, regional, or occupational personnel. Before the First World War these societies represented at most 10 percent of the French population (while at least half of Germans were directly covered), who tended to be an elite of the labor force, those who could and would maintain prompt payment of their monthly premiums. The neediest were neglected. Indeed, all persons extremely poor or chronically ill (especially TB patients) were ordinarily rejected for membership in a mutual society because they were likely to be a drain on its treasury. Many recorded cases testify that societies might eventually go bankrupt after one or several members contracted some prolonged and debilitating illness that required extensive funding unsustainable for a small local organization. It should be added that, besides the mutual aid societies and sometimes in conjunction with them, several industrial enterprises developed their own health plans for accident and illness, benefits that had been heretofore restricted to miners, railway workers, and some state functionaries. But these provisions likewise affected only a small minority of citizens.

Manifestly, the Third Republic's social needs were not being adequately addressed by these arrangements. Little wonder, therefore, that Alsace, returned to France after 1918 from nearly fifty years in the neighboring Reich, refused to relinquish the German system and pressured postwar French regimes to alter their ways. Herein lies an important explanation for the eventual curtailment of voluntarism and the conversion of France to the kind of welfare state that we associate with the Fourth and Fifth Republics. Alsace, as it proved during the interwar years, was to be a seedbed of German-style reforms.

The most egregious example of a voluntarist ethic in practice was the treatment of tuberculosis. That dreaded and seemingly incurable malady (before the introduction of antibiotics in the 1940s) took an estimated toll of one hundred thousand French lives every year during the entire tenure of the Third Republic. The severity of this epidemic would seem to require extreme measures. Yet the so-called "war on tuberculosis" was never more than a skirmish in France, marked by voluntary home medical care, the sale of special postage stamps, and heartrending dramatic performances by a fatally stricken Sarah Bernhardt on the Paris stage. Precisely what republican France did not implement was a mandatory program of medical screening, special hospital wards, and sanatorium treatment. Although loudly vaunted from Berlin, the curative impact of TB sanatoria was doubtless exaggerated, judging from the large number of relapses. Yet the mortality rate from consumption in France nearly doubled that of Germany. The scope of this tragedy was first revealed at the French Academy of Medicine in the 1890s, and it was still apparent between the two world wars despite efforts, abetted by the Rockefeller Foundation, to introduce a more stringent segregation of tubercular patients. Imperfect as it may have been, the sanatorium was certainly more effective than the spittoon in curbing the spread of Europe's most devastating infectious disease. Yet the public ethic of republican France continued to rest on the dubious notion that drastic state regulation of it was more suitable for Germanic than Gallic masses. As in the case of smallpox, the reluctance to adopt obligatory measures cannot be entirely explained by ignorance of their efficacy but by a willful decision to forego them in the name of individual liberty. Tuberculosis patients were thus free to die.

In sum, the conclusion is inescapable that a comprehensive system of social security, such as it was known in Germany since Bismarck, was virtually nonexistent before 1914 in republican France, where voluntarism remained the predominant trait of the public ethic. This record of feeble efforts was nevertheless not without redeeming qualities, if only to indicate a recognition of reformist concerns that pointed toward a more promising future. Laws of 1874 and 1892, for example, limited the hours of labor for women and children, mincing first steps on the long trail to an eight-hour day for all. In 1893 free medical assistance for the needy was guaranteed in an effort to extend medical care to the French countryside and to counter the localism that remained a principal impediment to national social reform. In 1898 a plan of no-fault accident insurance, like that of Germany, was introduced into industrial enterprises. A day of rest on the Sabbath was assured in 1906. And the year following saw the end of a Napoleonic provision that married women had no right to dispose of their own salary without written consent of their husband. Doubtless the most significant prewar legislation was a bill adopted in 1905 that required contributions by *patrons* and employees alike to a state social insurance plan to aid indigents who were old, infirm, or incurable—the first such enactment based on the incessantly debated and often stoutly resisted German principle of obligation. This measure was followed in 1910 by a pension plan, in frank imitation of the Bismarckian code of the 1880s, which offered retirement benefits for those over the age of sixty-five, again with mandatory participation of employers and workers. If that measure confirmed a clear advance in the theoretical embrace of obligation, its practical impact was limited by political controversy, legal restrictions (its wage withholding provision was struck down by the courts in 1912), and the hard fact that the current average life-expectancy for men was forty-eight, for women fifty-two. Finally, in 1913 the parliament supported a pronatal provision of assistance to large families, a movement that was to become more conspicuous in the wake of the First World War. The evidence shows that in all these matters republican France looked to the example of imperial Germany in framing social legislation. If this effort fell short, the deficiency was not due to the reformers' lack of information or interest in the German model but to a rather hopeless feeling that it was unattainable or unsuitable for French circumstances. Still, the larger picture was not entirely bleak, and the Third Republic may at least be credited with a social conscience that was conspicuously absent in regimes of the past.

The quotidian status of public health before and after 1914 is impossible to capture in firm statistics. True, the French population continued to be savaged by "the three scourges" (*les trois fléaux*) of tuberculosis, alcoholism, and syphilis. Yet some of the older infectious diseases that were big killers in the nineteenth century—such as cholera, typhus, and diphtheria—began to abate, and the national mortality rate slowly declined. In this regard, the notion of a Belle Epoque before the war is only partially mythical, notably because a general sense of prosperity after 1900 was encouraged by moderate increases in real wages. Rural France also seemed to thrive, although it did so by clinging to a patchwork of small independent landholdings that precluded much greater efficiency. Compared with Germany, French agriculture was consequently less productive, in part because of the German lead in chemicals and fertilizers. The result was, for instance, that wheat production per hectare in France was barely half that of Germany, foreshadowing a growing French deficit in international trade.

As for the social policy and performance of republican France, the years after 1918 brought some important advances. The return of Alsace-Lorraine, as noted, introduced in a concrete form the German health and welfare programs. The restored provinces refused to abandon their more generous entitlements, and through the French parliament they applied pressure on the nation to follow their example. Not directly related but complementary was the simultaneous extension of company health plans by *patrons* of French industrial enterprises. This growth was encouraged, in turn, by a resurgent pronatalist movement, which responded positively to the evident needs for increased manpower created by the dreadful losses of wartime. Above all, though harder to measure, there was also a growing realization among rural notables that local financial means were inadequate to deliver social assistance and that city fathers would have to look to the central state to fund the construction and maintenance of hospitals, clinics, pharmaceutical dispensaries, unemployment offices, and other welfare institutions.

Liberal reluctance to accept state intervention thus began to crumble, the best evidence of which was the 1928 and 1930 national insurance laws that pointed the way to a remarkable volte-face in public health and welfare after the Second World War. It should be kept in view, however, that during the entire Third Republic most of this legislation represented little more than a statement of greater expectations and good intentions rather than a solid record of accomplishment. Republican France, compared to Germany or Great Britain, was mainly engaged in an embarrassing effort of catch-up that offered an easy target for criticism by domestic opponents, who did not cease to afflict the national morale with charges that the state was apathetic and ineffectual in caring for its citizenry. Yet it did not prove easy to shake off the pervasive legacy of voluntarism. Not until July 1939, in the midst of national crisis, did the French parliament finally adopt a comprehensive *Code de famille* that incorporated fragments of previous social legislation. And even this delayed effort had serious drawbacks for many families, who saw their social security benefits in fact substantially reduced. It was a laudable gesture, no doubt, but—what else can one say?—too little, too late.

Chapter Four

A Flagging Demography

*E*verybody loves a mystery. Hence the statistical analysis of demographic patterns should be a favorite topic, because the rise and fall of certain population curves often defy totally rational explanation. Why, for example, did the French nation remain below forty million inhabitants before 1914 while imperial Germany was burgeoning to well over sixty million? Doubtless we shall never know the complete answer. Yet all parts of this conundrum are not equally perplexing, and it is important to gather the established data and to gain an overview of their implications.

Looking far back, it is evident that, from the latter decades of the Old Regime through the Napoleonic empire, the number of births in France was declining. Why? One obvious response, of course, is birth control. French parents evidently wanted fewer children, and they seized upon available means to prevent them. As before, coitus interruptus was the preferred method, but the use of condoms and diaphragms became increasingly widespread in the nineteenth century. The limitation of family size began before the Great Revolution with the aristocracy, a practice that thereafter spread steadily down the social scale as time passed. Plausibly, it has been asserted that this birth control served primarily to promote the ideal of a small inte-

gral bourgeois family, though that was surely a demographic phenomenon not distinctly French. What is clear, in any event, is that
the urge to avoid raising numerous children also began to affect the
artisanal and industrial working class, as well as—to a somewhat
lesser extent—rural families. Nowhere in Europe was this trend more
marked than in republican France.

It appears that a sudden demographic surge occurred right after
the Napoleonic wars, but it did not last. A national census in 1864
revealed that births exceeded deaths at that time in all of France by
only 145,000, that is, at an annual rate of merely 3.8 per thousand.
After 1870 this moderate growth became a pronounced slump. Following a war that was decisive but not extraordinarily costly in lives
lost, the relation of natality to mortality was barely breaking even.
Thereupon, the decade of the 1880s became the black hole of
French demography. In 1891 and 1892, for the first time, there was
an absolute population deficit, which was repeated in 1900, 1907,
and 1911. In numbers, republican France continued to skitter on
the edge of a national decline. Apparently, for many French parents
the notion of a Belle Epoque meant, among other things, changing
fewer dirty diapers in the middle of the night.

The long-term consequences of birth control were disturbing.
Despite a slight drop in infant mortality and in death from some infectious diseases, the French population was aging. At the same time,
the labor force was slow to evolve: before 1914 two-thirds of French
workers were still in old trades (textiles, alimentation, construction)
and only 12 percent in new industries (like metallurgy and chemicals).
The majority of French citizens continued to live in the countryside:
in 1911 more than 22 million resided in thirty-five thousand rural
communes, while only 17.5 million occupied cities—even when measured by the ridiculously low urban criterion of two thousand inhabitants. This rural-urban balance did not finally tip until the early
1930s. Not surprisingly, then, the industrial labor force at ages fifteen to sixty grew barely 17 percent between 1866 and 1906. Compared to the much more rapid urban and industrial development of
Germany and Great Britain, France was visibly bringing up the rear.
A single statistic tells it all: before 1914, fifty German cities had a
population over one hundred thousand; in France there were but five.

Precisely this sort of comparison with the German Kaiserreich was at the origin of France's fashionable prewar discussion of national "decadence," which now provided so much fodder for the boulevard press. What could be more alarming than to learn that, in the early 1890s, for every ten French births there were twenty-two German births? Or, in other terms, that during the two decades before 1910 the French population was increasing on an average of sixty-three thousand annually, the German population by five hundred thousand? The bulk of that increase west of the Vosges, it must be added, came through immigration. Hence, between the wars of 1870 and 1914, republican France had at most a demographic increment of 11 percent, leaving a total population that remained below forty million. In the meanwhile, Germany grew by 80 percent to a nation of nearly 66 million. These numbers could be twisted and turned at will (and they still can be), but the depressing image of a French populace dropping ever farther behind was much the same.

The Great War made matters far worse. All those who have studied and pondered the immense French losses draw a similarly dismal portrait of the resulting interwar demography. In 1918 republican France had 1.4 million dead to mourn and 1.1 million invalids to nourish. The number of unborn children as a result of the conflict is more difficult to estimate, but it surely exceeded a million; in addition to which one must count those civilians who died from other causes, including a deadly influenza epidemic at war's end. All in all, we may safely assume a French demographic deficit in excess of three million absent souls. Even by including the 1.9 million added with the return of Alsace-Lorraine, the net result left French citizens still far short of rising above the mythic threshold of forty million. Let it be added that, while German war casualties were greater in absolute numbers, France's relative loss exceeded that of any other nation in Europe: thirty-four per thousand French versus thirty per thousand Germans.

Disproportionately, of course, the main deficit was in the male population. France was consequently left with seven hundred thousand widows and eight hundred thousand orphans—numbers of individual tragedy that are beyond comprehension. Available men were thus scarce, meaning a postwar decline in marriages and births.

Other demographic side effects of the war were less obvious. There was a sharp increase in the divorce rate, presumably because of tensions produced by prolonged separation. Also the childbearing per married couple further receded, perhaps as much as 10 percent. Accordingly, by one reckoning, the French birth rate dipped from 20.7 per thousand in 1921 to 14.6 by 1936. Such estimates naturally vary from source to source, but the consensus is consistent with a general conclusion that republican France was hard put to recover any demographic vitality during the interwar years. During the entire decade of the 1920s, by that most telling of standards, French births exceeded deaths by less than one hundred thousand a year, and in the year 1929 the nation again registered an absolute population deficit. If the 1930s showed a slight improvement, the disturbing fact remained that, on an annual average, almost three times as many German babies were born in the ten years before 1940 as French.

Besides all of the above, statistics on mortality dropped less in France than elsewhere. The blame is ordinarily ascribed to a greater toll of alcoholism and, more concretely, to a relative lack of public health facilities. The most alarming result was a rate of death from tuberculosis that remained nearly double that of Germany throughout the interwar years. French youngsters and adults were more vulnerable to fatal disease, the long-range effects of which must ultimately be measured in terms of fewer pupils, laborers, and soldiers. Yet the chief victim of all was French self-confidence. Altogether indicative of that loss was the career of France's most illustrious demographer of the day, Jacques Bertillon, who in 1896 founded *L'alliance nationale pour l'accroissement de la population française,* an organization whose hopeful title indicated a clear purpose to promote greater social fecundity. But in 1911 Bertillon published a volume called *La Dépopulation,* which plotted the persistent French tendency to limit family size and sounded a note of alarm about the nation's extraordinarily high (albeit unverifiable) rate of abortion. He thereby coined an expression of concern that was to resonate during the rest of the Third Republic. After the demographic disaster of the First World War, his followers regrouped under the notably more defensive and pessimistic title of *L'alliance nationale contre la dépopulation*—as if the most that republican France could henceforth imagine was to avert a total relapse.

If there is one proposition on which all historians of the Third Republic agree, it is the lasting impact of the national trauma between 1914 and 1918. This ghastly collective memory was cultivated wherever one looked: in Paris, the eternal flame under the Arch of Triumph; the monuments to the dead in every French village across the land; the countless celebrations and demonstrations by veterans, most conspicuously on the annual national observance of Armistice Day; the plaques and crosses in every cemetery; and, not least, the swath of destruction in northeastern France, where fields and shattered towns lay for years in ruin. Meanwhile, scenes of war and destruction were being vividly depicted many times over in novels and films. To comprehend postwar France, drenched as it was with both patriotism and pacifism, we need to keep in view this enormous psychological burden. Therein lay the basis of an alliterative emotional progression, already suggested by the hard and irreducible demographic numbers, from decadence to depopulation to defeatism.

Chapter Five

A STAGNANT ECONOMY

A group of French economists and economic historians has recently published a collective volume concerning their nation's performance in the late nineteenth century. This anthology leads to a conclusion that the label of a "long stagnation" is altogether appropriate as a characterization of that time. Real dispute among the participants occurs solely on the issue of chronology: whether France's economic lethargy before the First World War was fairly brief, from the early 1880s to the mid 1890s, or whether it lingered over a much longer span from the late 1860s to 1905. This must rank as a loaded question like the proverbial when-did-you-stop-beating-your-wife? No matter what periodization they individually favor, the consensus of these experts remains that the Third Republic experienced a protracted slump in economic growth before 1914, the lasting effects of which continued to hamper French commerce and industry thereafter.

There is much statistical evidence to support this evaluation, although, as with all general theories, troublesome defects of it are exposed upon closer examination. It is well to begin by waiving the question of chronology. That a sort of depression ensued for a decade after the collapse of the Freycinet Plan in 1882 is beyond question. But the failure of that large program of government investment in public works, principally harbor facilities and secondary railroads, was also symptomatic of an enduring financial unsteadiness of republican France that can be detected both before and after its most critical phase. The fiscally overextended Second Empire in the 1860s should take some of the blame, including the costly war of 1870. France did not enjoy another period of sustained prosperity and expansion until the last prewar decade before 1914, whereupon a second expensive European conflict toppled the national economy once more into a vat of red ink. All things considered across the long duration of its existence, the Third Republic continued to suffer from a chronic weakness that precluded robust economic health.

Whether that condition should be called stagnation is nonetheless moot. At least three caveats need to be registered. First, the term is much too tepid to describe the decade of the 1880s. It was not that the French economy then decelerated to a walk; it stumbled and was set back. One clear example was public transportation, especially railways, which underwent a serious downsizing by reducing service, laying off workers, and suppressing orders for new rolling stock. Commerce, agriculture, and industry were consequently diminished. Second, the concept of stagnation would seem to imply a total lack of movement over a long term. But republican France was in many ways changing. Again, the evolution of the railway industry is illustrative. Transportation became vastly more democratized in the late nineteenth century. True, company profits did not rise dramatically, despite the notable influx of new passengers, in part because round-trip tickets and monthly *abonnements* cut into the proceeds. Nor did the fleet of steam locomotives greatly increase, largely because a new generation of more powerful engines was replacing the old, which were retired. Thus heavier loads of freight or passengers could be hauled by fewer trains. Faster, cheaper, and more efficient commerce by rail does not make a convincing argument for a stagnant economy. Third, while a virtual paralysis may have enveloped certain economic sectors, others visibly prospered. Some of the French textile industry was lost with Alsace, for instance, but the northern region around Roubaix thrived. Production of coal and coke rose, although not enough to meet demand, requiring imports that were themselves an indication of gradually renewed economic activity. An epidemic of phylloxera temporarily repressed wine production in large areas of southwestern France, but the per capita consumption of alcohol (and hence alcoholism) was up, and the industry rebounded before 1900. Harvests of grain and quantities of milled flour fluctuated, but that probably had more to do with the weather than with the stagnation of average growth rates. All in all, when viewed in sufficient detail, the economy of the early Third Republic was not as static as the hindsight of some theoreticians would suggest.

Not until this complex experience is placed into a comparative context, however, do the reasons for the French self-perception of a floundering economy come fully into focus. Again, a leading sector of every European nation, public transportation, provides a number of telling clues. Between 1870 and 1900, France's main northern seaport at Le Havre gained only slightly less than a million tons of shipping—not too bad, one might suppose, except that Hamburg's sea trade meanwhile rose by more than six times that amount, and those of Antwerp and Rotterdam by at least five times. Even tiny Bremerhaven was then handling nearly twice as many bales of raw cotton as Le Havre. Freight delivered by water passed immediately onto rails. By century's end, the weight of goods carried on German tracks averaged almost 300 million tons annually, whereas the French tonnage barely exceeded 100 million a year. The Kaiserreich's annual gross income from railway freight reached more than a billion Marks; French receipts were about half of that amount.

In regard to heavy industry—meaning primarily coal and steel— France also failed to keep pace. Lack of combustible fuels had long been a drag on the French economy and, despite increased production, it remained so. By the year 1910 French mines were extracting 38 million tons annually, but the nation still needed to import a third of its consumption. German output meanwhile reached 152 million tons of coal a year (nearly five times the French rate!), enough to sustain its own industry and yet to export large quantities, among others, to France. As for steel, French production doubled between 1896 and 1913, a remarkable accomplishment, yet the German lead in Europe was not remotely threatened. In the 1870s France had produced nearly 14 percent of the world's total of steel, Germany

18 percent; but on the eve of the First World War, those figures were respectively 8 percent and 29 percent. The reality was a growing industrial gap that fed French fears and German ambitions.

In metallurgy there were some bright spots. As every tourist to Provence knows, France was particularly rich in bauxite, with a consequence that before 1914 it stood second only to the United States in the production of aluminum. In turn, the technological advance in light metals helped to spur the fledgling industries of both automobiles and aircraft. Yet these innovations occurred in a context of artisanal enterprise and did not represent a conversion to huge and efficient industrial factories. If one searches for an explanation of France's relatively modest growth rate in the prewar years, it is to be found in structural differences, of which three are most striking: a much more restrained role of the republican state compared to imperial Germany; far less direct participation of credit banking in industry; and a virtual absence of the unfettered cartelization so characteristic of German manufacturers. To put the matter quite simply: France had no Ruhr. Instead, a host of light industries tended to cluster in and around Paris. In 1908, only sixteen French departments exceeded the national average of wealth, and all but one of them were located in the vicinity of the capital.

The greater extension and ever gathering density of Germany's industrial complex left the impression that republican France was at best running in place. One compensation was the concurrent French colonial expansion. Between 1870 and 1914 that domain increased from one to eleven million square kilometers with a population up from five to fifty million, a feat unmatched. But these numbers did not translate into commensurate economic benefits nor alter the fact of German commercial domination on the Continent. Before 1914, colonial possessions constituted barely 10 percent of French trade, small consolation for an inability to compete successfully for exports in the home European market. One example stands out, namely Germany's industrial production of steam locomotives, which far outstripped the French in some years by the astounding proportion of a tenfold or more. The decade of the 1880s proved to be a disaster. Whereas French private railway firms acquired a record of 741 engines in 1882, they purchased only 44 in 1888. French locomotive production correspondingly declined. Only 51 steam engines left the nation's industrial plants in 1887, 39 in 1888, and 26 in 1889. Germany's manufacturing firms in the meanwhile combined to reach an annual average rate of new locomotives that approached 700, more than enough to meet its national requirements. As a result, when the French rail companies suddenly required new machines to meet commercial demands created by the economic upturn after 1905, a third of them had to be imported from Germany. While the German metal and machine industries thereby gained control of the export market of continental Europe, the prewar foreign trade of such goods by republican France was confined mainly to its colonies.

France's wartime expenses were off the chart. Despite measures like starting an income tax, raising indirect revenues, and issuing savings bonds, the national treasury incurred a staggering annual deficit, which has been loosely estimated for the years 1914–1918 at seven times the entire 1913 budget. The long conflict with Germany thereby resulted inexorably in the fall of the franc and the rise of inflation, both to be indelible traits of the interwar economy. The obvious solution was to borrow cash, mostly from the United States and Great Britain. The magnitude of this war debt is difficult to fathom, but it is generally supposed to have reached 80 billion francs— and, if so, that was a sum equivalent to sixteen years of the ordinary prewar budget. As more than one economic historian has remarked, such dizzying math was actually understood by no one, not even those responsible for it.

The immediate postwar years brought further inflation. In the early 1920s prices were more than twice their prewar level. Meanwhile, the steep slide of the franc continued. Before the war it had traded regularly at 25.5 per British pound sterling. By 1924 the franc was pegged at 125, thus having lost nearly four-fifths of its earlier value. One must imagine the personal impact of these raw numbers on the French population. Coal for heating was scarce and expensive. Basic foodstuffs like sugar, butter, eggs, and meat became ruinously expensive. If the simultaneous collapse of the German currency seemed more dramatic, the French did not neglect to suffer. As for the macroeconomic situation, most experts favored a devaluation at least on the order of 35 to 40 percent. But political considerations dictated that the government maintain the franc, thereby attempting to create an illusion of normalcy. Few were fooled.

The fragility of state finances became, unavoidably, a matter not only of national but of international concern about the reparations clause of the Versailles Treaty. Oversimplified but essentially true, the problem remained that France was demanding 230 billion francs whereas Germany claimed that it could not scrape together more than 30 billion. How to deal with a recalcitrant Weimar Republic that threatened at any moment to disintegrate? That was the question that essentially dominated French domestic and foreign policy after 1918: whether to pursue a hard line of strict enforcement or to adopt a compromise (backed by the British). Was it nobler to accommodate the Germans and seek their integration into the European comity of nations or to squeeze them into compliance? No issue so categorically divided republican France and so accurately mirrored the shifting mood of its people. "The Germans will pay," endlessly muttered the Ministry of Finance. But others were unsure, and appeasement thus had its French patrons long before that word became an opprobrium.

The key figure of the 1920s was Raymond Poincaré. Born in eastern Lorraine near the German border, in 1870 he had as a child of ten fled with his family from the invading German army. Upon their return to the small town of Bar-le-Duc, they found it occupied for the next three years by "the Prussians," as the boy always preferred to call them for effect. Poincaré's rise in politics was colored by that experience and by the conviction that firmness was France's only recourse. Such an attitude accorded well with the revival of nationalism that swept the country during the Moroccan crises of 1905 and 1911, provoked by Germany's unwarranted intervention into French colonial affairs. It was therefore appropriate that Poincaré became President of the Republic shortly before the World War, and it was he, rather *malgré lui,* who then called Georges Clemenceau to the premiership during the decisive hour of the struggle. After the war, Poincaré returned to politics as the prime minister and was responsible for a decision to send more French troops into the Rhineland and Ruhr in 1923. Appalled by the ensuing obliteration of the

German Mark, he adopted a canon of fiscal austerity, which included budget cuts and tax increases. These sensible actions halted the rapid erosion of the franc, but also, in effect, they ended a policy of strict enforcement of reparations.

The results were various and complex, the stuff of countless diplomatic histories of the interwar years. First came the Dawes Plan of 1924, which attempted to aid the restabilization of the German economy by allowing for modest, slowly increasing reparations payments for five years before reaching a definitive settlement—an implicit renunciation of France's original demands. This made possible a period of so-called collective security marked by a Franco-German rapprochement under the Locarno agreement and the Weimar Republic's entry into the League of Nations, all of which culminated in the Kellogg-Briand peace pact of 1928. It was a good show. Moreover, both the French and German economies did in fact recover some stability. Through the 1920s France could boast a growth rate of 5 percent, which produced a national revenue in 1929, the peak year, that was a third above the level of 1913. A most-favored-nation arrangement between France and Germany meanwhile promoted French exports of agricultural products and raw materials in exchange for German machines, chemicals, and electronic equipment. Accordingly, the French trade deficit was slowly but steadily reduced. Poincaré's crowning achievement, and his swan song as it proved, was at last to obtain a major devaluation of the franc in June 1928—at, let it again be noted, only one-fifth of its prewar value.

All of these events played out on the surface of public life. Beneath them was a development barely perceived, and often denied, that forced republican France to lose further control of its destiny. There was no way to prevent a German recovery (nor an interest in doing so), no way to collect anything near the total reparations bill, no way to persuade an American president to waive the war debts, and no way to go it alone in a European community committed to collective security. Above all, there was no way to prevent the international financial turbulence that struck pitilessly in the autumn of 1929 and abruptly plunged every economic calculation into chaos.

The delayed effect in France of the Great Depression after 1929 recalled that of the Krach of European stock markets in 1873. With its self-sufficient agriculture and largely artisanal industry, the French economy seemed at first to be somewhat insulated against the more catastrophic impact felt by others. But if a broad recession was belated, it soon became smothering and lasting. First came three years of uncertainty, during which structural problems of the economy slowly emerged. The Young Plan of 1929 was supposedly to frame a definitive settlement of the reparations imbroglio, but its terms rapidly became irrelevant. They were never implemented and Germany never paid. Yet the *quid pro quo* of that agreement did matter, because it included the promise by France of a premature evacuation of the Rhineland. The last French troops left Koblenz and Mainz by early 1930, five years ahead of the schedule stipulated at Versailles. Like some oversized sea turtle stranded on a beach, France withdrew into its shell. Construction of the Maginot Line was completed, a reduction to one-year military service was adopted, and a moratorium on financial payments (proposed by Herbert Hoover) was accepted. Everything was in the passive voice. His health failing, Raymond Poincaré, the last symbol of defiance and stability, departed. In his stead, international negotiations were conducted by the more pliable Pierre Laval. The Lausanne conference of 1932 was thus a fitting sham, in reality signaling French acquiescence in a deterioration of circumstances beyond recall. Enter Adolf Hitler.

Already by 1934 signs of the times were scrawled on every wall in republican France. More than a million newly unemployed had materialized since late 1929. Prices were falling but so were incomes, as deflation gnawed at bourgeois savings accounts. Coal production was off by a quarter, agriculture and metallurgy by a third, and exports by 60 percent. Public life was scarred by scandals, demonstrations, strikes, and riots. All in all, France's industrial output fell by a fourth in the decade before 1939. Reducing the workweek further enfeebled the national economy without, as hoped, curbing unemployment. Unable to impede either the sudden collapse or the subsequent recovery of its neighbor in the 1930s, republican France was also helpless to avert its own gradual decline. One instance was indicative. After gathering international support, the French were able in 1931 to block a proposed merger of the German and Austrian economies, a fusion declared to be incompatible with the Treaty of

Versailles. But this maneuver proved to be merely a finger in the dike, and it was not long before everyone was obliged to add another German term to the common vocabulary: *Anschluss.*

Chapter Six

A SEXIST TRADITION

*I*n more than one regard, the Bonapartist legacy continued to weigh on France, and nowhere more so than in the relationship between the sexes. Allegedly, the Napoleonic Code established equality before the law. Yet women could not vote or hold political office, and the denial of women's suffrage throughout the entire span of the Third Republic was only the first in a long list of social restrictions that persisted in practice. Male domination remained the rule from beginning to end. Viewing this record, feminist scholars—simply meaning those who specialize in the history of women—tend to waver between the poles of lamentation and celebration. That is, either they deplore the unblushing social discrimination that everywhere condemned the female gender to an inferior status, or they praise the long-suffering and unrelenting progress of the distaff sex led by a few remarkable individuals. Of course, there is some evidence to support both standpoints. Yet even the most balanced overall evaluation of this aspect of the Third Republic's institutional tenure must insist on a deeply engrained male bias that radically limited the role of women in French society.

Republican France did allow some advance for females, notably in public education. Under the Ferry Laws, adopted in the 1880s, many

41

new schools for girls were opened across the land and thousands began flocking to them. The rate of literacy for women had previously lagged behind that of men, and the gap started to close. However, this development may be seen in either of two quite different perspectives: as a tentative step toward women's liberation or as the conditioned reflex of reigning male elites to keep women in their place. Again, if something is to be said for both, the evidence mainly supports the latter. The most convincing proof lies not in ringing orations on feminine virtue by republican politicians at graduating exercises of the *écoles de filles,* but in an examination of the structure of their curriculum. In 1893, for instance, a program of moral education for girls' primary classes was drafted. It was to be similar to that for boys except for the emphasis on "certain particular duties" of females, including the chores of homemaking. Instruction for young women in secondary education would center not on *"lutte pour la vie,"* as for boys, but on *"concorde pour la vie."* Perhaps more revealing still was a curricular proposal containing a clause, for girls only, about "the eminent virtues of silence." True, this expression was eventually deleted, yet republican legislators arguably favored it less in theory than in practice. In any event, the preponderance of documentation falls squarely on the side of continuing male supremacy in public education well into the twentieth century, a barrier of benighted attitudes that only a relatively few extraordinary women were able to breach. Several distinguished names in the arts and sciences from George Sand to Marie Curie to Simone de Beauvoir did not alter this underlying reality.

A few statistics on female lycées are revealing. Dating back to the days of Victor Duruy, Minister of Education under the Second Empire, these schools numbered 23 by the mid 1880s, 70 at the turn of the century, and 138 in 1913. Thus in all, nearly thirty-three thousand young French women were receiving a secondary education by the outbreak of the First World War (in a nation, we recall, of forty million). That was some progress. But the caveat bears repeating that their curriculum was specifically designed for females, who were usually offered no courses in ancient philosophy or classical languages, the staples of male lycées. Instead, they were taught modern literature, home crafts, and moral lessons—not always the most useful subjects as preparation for the required baccalaureate exam that provided entry to the university. Some nonetheless succeeded. The number of women attending French universities rose fourfold in the two decades before 1914 to about 2000 (barely a tenth of male students). Only a handful, however, were admitted to the faculties of law or medicine, and none took up engineering.

No less significant was the positive evolution of social reform and public health under the republican regime. The great majority of persons receiving what we might call welfare benefits, meaning state-funded public assistance of some sort, were women. One principal explanation of this statistical imbalance was apparently the longer life expectancy of females, because nearly half of all the beneficiaries were widowed. The other most conspicuous category was unwed mothers. Alone, destitute, and often unemployed, a woman was far more often than not the recipient of modest state aid. Nevertheless, a study of the records of reform committees, social agencies, and private physicians (including the French Academy of Medicine) demonstrates that the actual input of women was almost totally negligible. Grotesque as it may now appear to us, it was not uncommon for a caucus of ten to fifty elderly gentlemen—without a single woman present—to discuss in detail such matters as breast-feeding, birth control, abortion, prostitution, and venereal disease. They invariably shared the common view that women were feeble, unable to compete with men in the marketplace, and thus in need of protection and public assistance. Females were thought to be less durable, more subject to fatigue that adversely affected their daily performance on the job and their nightly aptitude for reproduction. Male reformers generally concurred that a woman's place was in the home and that factory labor for them was somehow unnatural and degrading at the least or an unfortunate necessity at best.

Yet women were entering the labor force after 1870 in unprecedented numbers. An interesting example was the railway industry. At first glance, it appears that railroads were entirely a man's universe throughout the Third Republic. Executives, chairs of the board, chiefs of operations, stationmasters, engineers and firemen and conductors, construction workers and repairmen—all were males. But women there were, present at the creation of the industry and increasingly numerous in its ranks. Unfortunately, they are visible to us only through a veil of imperfect data. Take the women who were employed from the outset of the railway age to clean the interior of passenger cars at journey's end. Because they were regarded by the private French railway companies basically as domestic servants, possessing no special training or skill, they were not accorded a regular status as railway employees and did not usually appear in company records. Literally, they just did not count. Another important representation in this initial tide of female employees were those, often uniformed, who stood at level crossings to make certain that the gates were closed and that any approaching road traffic was alerted to the arrival of a train. Until the late 1880s, nearly half of all women salaried by French railway administrations performed this function as "flag ladies." After the turn of the century they would be largely replaced by automatic gates and electric signals, and they became technologically obsolete.

About the same time, however, a second wave arrived with the introduction of the typewriter. In addition to cleaning, signaling, selling tickets, operating telegraphs, and attending bookstalls in stations, women could henceforth be found handling correspondence, keeping financial ledgers, dispatching freight, and even in exceptional cases overseeing small stations. The railway industry, in short, was becoming highly bureaucratized, for which the employment of women was essential. Yet company archives show, not too surprisingly, that the most important motive for hiring females was that they were cheap labor. To cite a single instance in 1885, twenty of forty-two railway employees on a spur line in eastern France were women, who together were paid 9420 francs annually. If all of these posts had been occupied by men, their estimated total compensation would have been 26,040 francs. Thus the employment of women saved the rail company exactly 16,620 francs a year on one lone stretch of track. If we multiply that figure by several thousand all across the nation, there can be no mystery why French railway executives turned to female labor.

Exact statistics on hiring are an illusion. But the consensus of research is that, during the late nineteenth century, between 7 and 10 percent of French railway employees were women. The documentation is unambiguous that they ordinarily held the most menial positions. Their pay was low, their hours long, and their opportunity to obtain a raise, a bonus, or a promotion virtually nil. Yet their numbers were sufficient to require some regulation and to raise disciplinary concerns. In these matters it was the mostly state-operated German railroads that took the lead and offered models for the private French companies. Female employees should be of "good reputation." They could be better controlled as well as protected when segregated into separate working areas with their own entrance. "It has happened often enough," as one German editorial commented with an unintended double entendre noted in France, "that intelligent young girls had to be dismissed because their moral standards left something to be desired." To be sure, women were often credited by male supervisors with "extraordinary cleverness" in performing manual tasks such as typing and bookkeeping, but as another editorial in a French railway journal also observed: "Women do not display the personal independence and the judgment that are necessary for some positions." Translation: girls make good secretaries.

A broader look at women's employment in French industry shows that their numbers rose from 1.5 million in 1876 to well over 2 million in the prewar years. By 1911, they accounted for nearly 37 percent of the industrial labor force, though their tasks were ordinarily at the bottom of the pay scale in older industries such as textiles, tobacco, and alimentation. To this total one must add at least a million servants, of which the large majority were women. This rise in female employment, already evident before the war of 1914 and notably accelerated by it, was not sustained during the interwar period. In 1913 the ratio of women to men holding industrial jobs was 58/100; by 1921 that figure was up to 61/100; but in 1930 it fell back to 54/100. Such a diminution can be ascribed mostly to a decline of the French textile industry after 1918. It also reflected a more general trend toward greater mechanization that eliminated much labor-intensive handwork often performed by females. In addition, after 1929, France's growing unemployment rate could not fail to hurt women and immigrants first of all. An estimated three hundred thousand female workers were laid off between 1931 and

1936. Consequently, the main occupation of women remained house-keeping, a demanding enough task at a time when washing machines, vacuum cleaners, and refrigerators were beyond the reach of most family budgets.

For women, as usual, the devil was in details. A law in 1884 legalized divorce, but this enactment created a right seldom exercised in a society in which it was, to say the least, discouraged. As mentioned, late nineteenth-century legislation restricted the working day for females and children to eleven hours, and in 1900 the Loi Millerand reduced the limit from eleven to ten, in fact a minimal amelioration that largely ratified the existing practice. Similarly, a bill was passed by the French parliament in 1909 that guaranteed a maternity leave of eight weeks for working women, but this provision was without a state subsidy for their support during that interim, making it a luxury that few could afford. Change came slowly, if at all. To cite another example, not until 1937 could a female spouse obtain a passport without permission of her husband. Yet the most symbolic and repressive restriction, hands down, was the lack of a vote. A favorable ballot in the Chamber of Deputies was overturned by the Senate, where fears lingered that the weaker sex would fall under the nefarious political influence of priests. Even more conspiratorial, and perhaps more to the point, senatorial worries persisted about the danger that urban masses, when strengthened by formerly deprived females, might soon overwhelm the rural notability. Hence women's suffrage would not be accorded until after the Second World War.

A conclusion based on such evidence is virtually redundant. To return first to a specific earlier theme, it is clear that construction of the railway industry—unquestionably the major technological innovation of the nineteenth century and still an indispensable commercial factor during the twentieth—resulted from the cooperation of state government, private capital, and civil engineering. All were exclusively male preserves. Women were marginal and in the minority among French railway employees, their contribution strictly limited by the structure of society and its existing educational establishment. Nor was the railway industry exceptional. The same circumstances demonstrably held for banking and big business like steel, chemicals, or electricity, as well as for the Church and of course the military.

Republican France did not basically differ from the rest of Europe in this respect, although it must be recorded that women's suffrage in Germany and Great Britain was introduced by 1919, decades before the first woman cast a ballot in France. Pressure to follow that example grew during the interwar years, and yet the democratic conventions of republicanism failed to foster a French suffragette movement of any great consequence. The Third Republic therefore ended, as it began, still bearing deep traces of Napoleonic sexism.

Chapter Seven

AN EDUCATED ELITE

*L*ike universal military conscription, compulsory public education
was a treasured republican principle. Both were considered to be
manifest signs of democracy, which, when fully realized, would separate the new era from France's autocratic past. Yet the curiosity was
that such measures had already been adopted by authoritarian Germany. In 1870 a German army of conscripts had soundly trounced
French professional soldiers in battle. And at the same time Germany could boast of a literacy rate that was among the highest in
Europe and certainly above that of France, where mandatory primary schooling was not yet the rule. In that sense, the wave of military and educational reforms under the Third Republic could be
said to pass not from West to East but from East to West.

The French, as always, were to do things in their own way. They
regarded the German educational model with a mixture of admiration and apprehension, fully recognizing its obvious virtues but re-
fusing for their own reasons to adopt a slavish imitation. This
reluctant disposition was best illustrated by attempts of some republican reformers to break the stronghold of a classical curriculum in
primary and secondary schools. They pointed to the system of *Real-
schulen* in Germany, which offered pupils a second scholastic track
that featured, rather than a concentrated dose of Greek and Latin, a

core of courses emphasizing modern languages, science, mathematics, and history. In Germany both tracks could lead to the university and, while classical training was not neglected in the standard *Gymnasium,* it no longer enjoyed a monopoly of access to higher education. This desirable arrangement, the French reformers contended, could be embodied in an *enseignement secondaire spécial* that would complement the traditional lycée. Thereby, for instance, the embarrassing scene might be avoided when a student entering medical school knew irregular Greek verbs by heart but had only the vaguest acquaintance with biology or chemistry. Logical as that proposal might have seemed, this reform movement achieved at most a very modest success in France. The reality was that the classical lycée—particularly those famous Parisian institutions like Henri Quatre and Louis Le Grand—prevailed with their superior prestige intact. To embark on a medical career throughout the Third Republic, a secondary graduate would ordinarily need to spend a preparatory (not to say remedial) year in the study of natural sciences. Thus, after 1870 as before, though with some modifications, the French elite would display first and foremost a classical formation. A physician, it was thought, should be a person of distinction, for which such an education was indispensable.

Statistics are a helpful albeit crude measure of republican progress in public education. After passage of the Ferry Laws in the early 1880s, some twenty thousand primary schools and nearly six hundred thousand pupils—for whom enrollment was now obligatory—were added during the next two decades. If it is therefore fitting to speak of a notable spike in the democratization of primary education, one must also record a much more halting evolution at the secondary level. Barely 1 percent of primary pupils reached the lycée. The number of young males enrolled in them increased from 155,000 in 1876 to only 170,000 by 1914. About 8,000 of these annually obtained a baccalaureate degree that permitted entrance to a university. The total of university students rose steadily but slowly from 10,000 in 1875 to 20,000 in 1900 and then to 42,000 by 1914.

The importance of Jules Ferry's reforms, let it be added, must be judged not only in terms of quantity but also of content. In addition to his educational programs, Ferry was reputed as a champion of

France's remarkable colonial expansion under the Republic. The common denominator of these two enterprises was his sense of a French "civilizing mission" to spread enlightenment at home and abroad. Particularly notable in that regard were the historical textbooks, widely distributed in national and colonial schools, authored by the renowned Sorbonne scholar Ernest Lavisse. After spending four years of study and research in Berlin during the early 1870s, Lavisse was uniquely qualified to present a viewpoint that was at once patriotic and perceptive about French vulnerability vis-à-vis Germany. Like so many intellectuals of the time, he displayed a proper respect for German efficiency and prowess, but he also found in these same qualities "reasons for apprehension." These conflicting attitudes, by all accounts, were deeply engrained in the three generations between the wars of 1870 and 1914—so much so that one exhaustive study of literary and historical writings during those years has convincingly summarized them as "the German crisis in French thought." If a certain reductionism permeates this thesis, it points undeniably to an identifiable characteristic of the Belle Epoque.

In republican France education was inextricable from religion. The military defeat of 1870 was followed by a religious revival, of which two symbols stood out: the construction of the striking basilica of Sacré Coeur on the bluffs of Montmartre overlooking Paris and the numerous pilgrimages to the shrine of Lourdes that gained immense popularity after completion of connecting railway lines to southern France. Initially there was in all of this commotion a tendency to confound Christianity with monarchy, and also to conflate clerical influence with conservative education. The larger issue, of course, was the dubious compatibility of a secular republican ethic with an established religious tradition. The Roman Church's reluctance to cede ground, especially in matters of educational reform, placed it awkwardly and increasingly in a crosscurrent to the strong convictions of laity professed under the banner of French republicanism. An attempted readjustment of the Vatican's antirepublican policy after the death of the ultraconservative Pope Pius IX and the ascension of Leo XIII was short-lived. This *ralliement* was in effect a declaration, most clearly stated in the papal encyclical *Rerum Novarum* in 1891, that the faithful might be at the same time Catholic and republican. The first result of Leo's pronouncement was to loosen ties of the Church to the extreme Right, which eventually led to an embarrassing condemnation by the Papacy of the *Action Française* in 1926.

Yet such a reconciliation was soon undercut by the Dreyfus Affair, which proved to be, as in so many respects, a critical psychological and political moment for the Republic. Once a young artillery officer was accused of leaking military secrets through the German embassy in Paris, the Church made a fateful choice to support members of the French *État-Major* who were, as it later came out, guilty of framing Captain Alfred Dreyfus, a German-speaking Alsatian Jew. The protracted clash between Dreyfusards and anti-Dreyfusards reanimated the old antagonisms of anticlericalism toward the Church and prompted a new surge against the Catholic clergy's participation in the public schools. Led by the avid Radical Émile Combes, who took up Georges Clemenceau's campaign of years past, republican France marched directly to the separation of Church and State in 1905. Among other things, this meant closing over three thousand Catholic schools, evicting hundreds of religious personnel from instructional posts in public education, and breaking off diplomatic ties with the Vatican. It was the high tide of republican *laïcité*. In the place of priests and nuns, accused of indoctrinating pupils with all manner of superstition, now stood a corps of *instituteurs* and *institutrices* who were charged with dispensing secular republican values instead.

Meanwhile, the German university system probably ranked at the top, along with the Prussian general staff, as an object of French admiration. The quantity and variety of institutions of higher education in Germany were dazzling. Whereas in 1890 about half of all French university students were packed into Paris, their German counterparts were enrolled in twenty-one centers of learning, nearly all of which boasted complete degree-granting faculties of philosophy, law, medicine, and theology. By contrast, immediately after the loss of Alsace in 1870, France had only three fully accredited medical schools in Paris, Montpellier, and Nancy (where the former Strasbourg faculty took refuge). Funding for these faculties was indicative. Before 1914 the medical budget of the new Kaiser-Wilhelms-Universität in

"Strassburg" was ten times that of its competing analogue in Nancy. Accordingly, while the former served as a conspicuous international showcase for the primacy of German scientific research, the latter played a more modest role merely as an academic observatory and an intellectual liaison between France and Germany.

With a larger budget, more students and professors, better physical facilities, and greater prestige, surely the German university structure merited imitation? But a literal adaptation of Germany's precedent in higher education presented republican France with serious and indeed insuperable difficulties. Before 1940, and well beyond, the essence of French university life remained its concentration within Paris, rather than a distribution among regions, as in Germany. The *grandes écoles* were a uniquely Parisian phenomenon, and entry into them represented the pinnacle of achievement for scores of French students from the provinces. To reach the top of one's chosen profession almost invariably required a diploma from the École Polytechnique, the École des Ponts et Chaussées, the École Supérieure des Mines, the École Normale Supérieure, the École Libre des Sciences Politiques, or some other elite institution located in the capital. Even the French military academy was conveniently situated in St.-Cyr, only a brief train ride from downtown Paris. Far too much intellectual and financial capital was already invested in this centralized arrangement for it to be overturned or significantly modified by a political regime so indecisive as the Third Republic.

The interwar years brought little change. But they did see a calming of the prewar religious turmoil and of its deleterious effects on public education. After all, the separation of Church and State could be seen, as it often was by wiser heads, as the end of the French Kulturkampf rather than its culmination. Such relaxation was aided after 1918 by the return of Alsace-Lorraine, where the Napoleonic Concordat was still in place (an anomaly permissible since 1870 under a decentralized German administration). Not that this transition went altogether smoothly: for one thing, there was the tacky problem of replacing German-speaking teachers and priests after a prolonged "occupation." One symptom of renewed harmony, nonetheless, was the restoration of relations with the Vatican, where the newly installed (in 1922) Pope Pius XI agreed in effect to appoint more liberal French bishops to ecclesiastical vacancies as a *quid pro quo* for republican concessions in the strict enforcement of secular legislation.

In turn, the gradual lessening of religious strife encouraged a further democratization of public education. By 1938 the number of pupils attending secondary lycées exceeded two hundred thousand. Two frequently cited caveats did not seriously diminish this advance of republican France. First, the increased enrollment occurred almost entirely in the cities, to the neglect of the still sizable rural population. And second, it did not diminish the rivalry between parochial and public schools, a distant echo of times and conflicts past. Still, all in all, French intellectual life in general and public education in particular were able to progress in their own fashion, perhaps overmatched in sheer quantity more than in actual quality by the nation's challenging neighbor.

Chapter Eight

A XENOPHOBIC STYLE

*N*o single episode during the seven decades of the Third Republic aroused such passions as the Dreyfus Affair. The arrest, court-martial, imprisonment, and eventual exoneration of a military subaltern charged with espionage for Germany has fascinated researchers and readers alike for generations. Unquestionably, one of the reasons for this notoriety is simply that the Affair was one of the great detective stories of the nineteenth century, complete with conspiratorial plots, courtroom drama, sensational headlines, forged documents, Devil's Island, and the rest.

Yet, if anything, interest in the fate of Alfred Dreyfus has risen, not declined, in the twentieth century. The fact that he was a Jew, falsely accused and cruelly mishandled, has made him an emblematic figure whose significance transcended his personal stature. Little wonder, after the Second World War and the revelations about Nazi extermination camps, that the Dreyfus Affair came to be seen in the lurid light of the Holocaust. Most notable among the many analysts, Hannah Arendt traced a direct line from the Affair to the origins of totalitarianism in Europe. Although there is no evident reason to abandon this approach altogether, it is now appropriate to place the Affair into a larger context.

The main factor that must be taken into account is that republican France was the first European nation to be seriously touched by a massive immigration. The number of foreign workers and their families within the French borders between 1850 and 1870 tripled to more than a million. By 1900 immigrants comprised at least 3 percent of the population, and rumors abounded that they were procreating at a much more rapid rate than the French themselves. For every thousand residents England had five immigrants, Germany six, and France twenty-three. One French social reformer estimated that the number of foreigners in France would, through immigration and reproduction, rise to ten million within the next half of a century. If so, in the likely event that the Republic's demographic curve remained depressed, they would constitute fully a quarter of the total French population by 1950. Fear of that eventuality—in a word, xenophobia—was palpable, and it has remained so ever since.

Many of the newcomers before 1914 were migrant laborers who accepted menial employment in agriculture and industry, usually in border areas. Italians tended to congregate around the busy Mediterranean ports of Marseille and Cette (now Sète); Belgians, in the northern textile and mining regions near Lille; Spaniards, on the adjacent southwestern fringes of the Midi. A fourth identifiable immigrant group of Germans was somewhat different. Although some remained on the eastern frontier, many took up residence in Paris and other French towns. These more widely dispersed Germanic types were, moreover, indistinguishable from the nearly one hundred thousand Alsatians who had opted for French nationality after 1870 and resettled west of the Vosges. Born in Mulhouse, Alfred Dreyfus, a young probationary artillery officer attached to the *État-Major*, was one of the latter.

Recent studies of neglected documents in French military archives have placed the general circumstances of the Affair into an altered perspective. They prove that the very same ranking military men who framed Dreyfus had long harbored xenophobic suspicions about German-speaking Alsatians, whose loyalty to republican France they considered to be dubious. Accordingly, they had already made elaborate preemptive plans to meet this menace in the case of an acute international crisis. The current Minister of War in the early 1890s,

General Auguste Mercier, and his chief of counterespionage in the Ministry's Second Bureau, Colonel Jean Sandherr (also from Mulhouse), conspired to draft two enemies lists: the so-called *Carnet A* for aliens of military age living in France, and *Carnet B* for those, French or foreign, suspected of being German agents. Precise instructions were drafted concerning the possible arrest of these persons, who would be—even lacking substantial evidence—treated as criminals and incarcerated without trial, solely on the Ministry's presumption of their guilt. For Mercier and Sandherr, there would be no distinction between indictment and conviction.

That was not all. Well before Dreyfus was taken into custody, Colonel Sandherr managed to solicit from army corps commanders exact information about preparations to herd these prisoners into detention camps in southern France. They would be apprehended and rounded up at a given alarm, shipped by rail to the camps, and held there under armed guard for the duration of the crisis. Authorities anticipated as many as 100,000 such cases, of which more than 30,000 would be in Paris, another 12,500 in Lyon, and over 10,000 in Nancy. The archival fragments that remain from the enemies lists contain about 2,500 names. Three-fifths of these were French, the rest immigrants. And, in disproportionate number, they conspicuously included many Alsatians.

When, in September 1894, an agent of the Second Bureau retrieved a curious document from the wastebasket of the German military attaché in Paris, listing confidential information apparently sent to the Germans by a French artillery officer, there was every inclination of military chiefs in the Ministry of War, who had been plotting the seizure of one hundred thousand suspects, to move against a single Alsatian named Alfred Dreyfus.

These details must somewhat qualify the conventional assumption that the origin of the Dreyfus Affair was an eruption of French anti-Semitism that became an immediate prelude to twentieth-century European fascism. Seen against a much larger backdrop of xenophobia, the character of republican France assumes a different aspect. True, an anti-Semitic streak became quickly apparent with the rabid publications of Édouard Drumont. But it should be remembered that Drumont was a compulsive eccentric who purposely distorted the case in order to justify a scurrilous theory, propounded only a few years before in *La France Juive*, according to which Jews were everywhere manipulating the Republic's politics and public institutions for their own benefit. Furthermore, let it be recorded that rumors of "pogroms" in France—unfortunately echoed by several contemporaries of Dreyfus and by some of his later biographers—have been wildly exaggerated. There appeared no serious well-organized popular anti-Semitic movement in France, nor was there (as in Germany) a self-designated anti-Semitic political party. Even in Algiers, scene of the most strident anti-Semitic campaign of the time, agitators failed to found a coherent and durable political faction. Surely the actual events of the Dreyfus Affair are sinister enough without ascribing them to a vast wave of anti-Semitism that supposedly swept across republican France.

However one evaluates the Affair as such, there is no doubt that the slow dissolution of the allegations against Dreyfus provoked hard feelings on all sides. We have already seen how these emotions infused the religious and educational controversies of the Third Republic, and there were other ramifications as well. It was not only that the nation was polarized because lines hardened between the political Left and Right. Also, parties on both sides of that hypothetical divide were seriously split. The most significant of such instances, later to be considered, concerned the Socialists: some of them, behind Jules Guesde, declared the scandal to be no more than an internecine dispute among the reigning French notability that was essentially irrelevant for the working class; whereas others followed Jean Jaurès in denouncing the villains for a moral violation of basic human rights. But equally affected, for example, was the alignment of moderate republicans, of whom one faction led by Jules Méline broke away to join the camp of anti-Dreyfusards. It is impossible to determine the degree to which that label deserves to be equated with anti-Semitism. Arguably what the two had in common was not a base racist instinct but a desire to defend the honor of the military establishment, whose undiminished capacity to defend the Republic against domestic and foreign (read: German) foes was felt to be more significant than the personal fortunes of a single individual. Be that as it may, in the public arena anti-Semitism became increasingly associated with the rightist extremes of nationalism, militarism, and clericalism. A plausible conclusion is therefore that positing the appearance of anti-Semitism is more crucial to explain the consequences of the Dreyfus Affair than to describe its origins.

Paramount among those long-term results was the formation of an antiparliamentary opposition to the republican consensus. This loose coalition essentially comprised three distinctive components: one on the Right (monarchists, Bonapartists, Boulangists, nationalists like Déroulède, then later fascists and Pétainists); another on the Left (Blanquists, Marxists, Guesdists, Communists, etc.); and a heterogenous group of "occasionalists" who perked up at every political crisis or public scandal from Panama (1892) to the Stavisky incident (1934). All of these elements were present in the Dreyfus Affair and, in one oddly melded permutation or another, they collectively hounded and finally weakened republican France through the 1930s.

It is unnecessary to linger here over a historiographical debate about the relatively quiescent decade of the 1920s. Some scholars have cited the silence of the *Ligue des patriotes* at that time and speculated that anti-Semitism (with the notable exception of the *Action Française*) declined after the rehabilitation of Dreyfus. Others contend that racist sentiment was always latent, in fact rampant, merely awaiting more favorable circumstances, and they can point to the creation in 1924 of another league, the *Jeunesses patriotes,* whose leader, Pierre Taittinger, was inspired by the takeover of Italy by Mussolini's blackshirts. Upon reflection, these subjective interpretations seem less self-contradictory than a first glance might suggest, and they unduly draw attention away from the larger underlying issue of xenophobia. The operative fact was that by 1930 the percentage of immigrants among the French population had more than doubled since 1914, from about 3 percent to nearly 7 percent—that is, a total of more than three million foreigners. In addition, republican France housed over three hundred thousand naturalized citizens. These ranks were swelled by a post-1918 wave of Polish immigration, which supplanted Belgian and Spanish aliens as second in quantity to the Italians. In these statistics of *Gastarbeiter* and their families was fodder enough to feed old xenophobic fears in France, quite apart from the rather marginal activity of anti-Semitic agitators.

A sudden shift of the public mood or policy is hard to connect with the advent of Nazism in 1933. Little was yet known of Adolf Hitler, and the French had little reason at that moment to suppose that he, apparently just another chancellor of the Weimar Republic, would long survive. That illusion was slow to evaporate. It still nourished hopes for the Munich agreement in 1938. But by then it was at least becoming clear that three million immigrants residing in France mattered far less than the mass of more than seventy million Germans within easy earshot.

Chapter Nine

A SOCIALIST REVIVAL

*T*he Socialist movement in nineteenth-century Europe had many faces. Among them, with its concentrated heavy industry and huge organized labor force, German Social Democracy was clearly preeminent. One source of this strength was that the SPD could boast of a single ideological point of reference: the revolutionary writings of Karl Marx. Programmatically at least, a more moderate strain represented by the state-oriented stance of Ferdinand Lassalle was recessive. French Socialism differed in some important respects, partly because its intellectual roots were so heterogenous. Including, among others, Babeuf, Fourier, Saint-Simon, Blanqui, Louis Blanc, Proudhon, as well as Marx, the pantheon of leftist theoreticians was infinitely variable, a mantle of many colors. Nor did one size fit all. It is not surprising therefore that the Socialist tradition of republican France often seemed to lack coherence. In a nation of landholding peasants and artisanal trades, moreover, the movement remained relatively weak in numbers when compared—as it usually was, unfavorably—to its German counterpart.

All strands of French Socialism were present in body or spirit during the Paris Commune, when, individually and collectively, they came to grief. The decade of repression that followed virtually erased all leftist organizations from the political map. A gradual rehabilitation could occur only after the amnesty granted to communards in 1880 took effect. Obviously, this rebirth of Socialism in France must be an essential element in any history of the Third Republic. When divided inevitably into two phases, before and after the First World War, that tale was dominated by a pair of formidable personalities: Jean Jaurès and Léon Blum. Despite the fundamentally different circumstances under which they presided over their party, there were evident strands of continuity between the two. One of these, which it is possible to emphasize here without forcing the evidence, was their intense preoccupation with Germany. In that respect, finally, neither had much choice.

Originally Jaurès intended to become an academic. Born deep in the Midi, he gravitated to the University of Toulouse, where he wrote his doctoral thesis on the origins of German Social Democracy. In this work Jaurès dissented from Marx's catastrophic version of social evolution, finding him simply to be "superannuated" now, in late century, when France was republican and real wages for workers were rising. Reform, not revolution, was the wave of Europe's future. No less overtly than Eduard Bernstein in Germany, Jaurès thus became a frank revisionist; and, like Bernstein, he identified himself as a neo-Kantian insofar as he emphasized the moral content of Socialist doctrine. Such an orientation proved to be crucial in the Dreyfus Affair, as we saw, when Jaurès opposed the more orthodox Marxist position of his rival Jules Guesde and drew a large faction of his Socialist comrades to the Dreyfusard cause. It was a critical moment, when human rights prevailed over revolutionary creeds, and it cleared the way for Jaurès later to claim leadership of a united French Socialist party (SFIO).

This eminence did not come easily, nor was it ever free of controversy. Besides the residual factionalism within his party, Jaurès had constantly to contend with an autonomous cadre of trade unions, the *Conféderation Générale du Travail* (CGT), inheritor of the independent *Bourses du Travail* founded in 1886 by the late Fernand Pelloutier. Pelloutier's vague threat of a general strike was passed on to the CGT and became a staple item in its repertoire of intransigence. Jaurès was consequently in no position at century's end to control an ever swelling undercurrent of strikes. In 1895 France lost an estimated 600,000 work days through these stoppages; in 1900 that number was 3,500,000. Maximalist in outlook, French syndicalism thereby became inapt for compromises and remained an unflagging challenge to the kind of Socialist reformism within the republican consensus that Jaurès continued to advocate.

All of which was vastly and unavoidably complicated by the German connection, again and again manifested at a series of international Socialist conclaves. At a Paris congress in 1900 Jules Guesde was backed by the eminent Karl Kautsky in opposing support by Jaurès for participation by a Socialist deputy, Alexandre Millerand, in a bourgeois cabinet (which included a general who had helped suppress the Commune in 1871). Four years later, at another gathering in Amsterdam, Kautsky was joined by SPD veterans August Bebel and Wilhelm Liebknecht in demanding that the French Socialists put their house in order by forming a united party—which, on the surface, they did in 1905 by founding the SFIO. If Jaurès surpassed Guesde in the process, he could not escape criticism that his following lacked the solidarity and clear proletarian outlook of the SPD.

These problems became more acute after the First Moroccan Crisis of 1905, the effect of which was to pit pacifism against nationalism, a common shorthand formula for stating the German question. The Socialist congress at Stuttgart in 1907 revealed deep fault lines in the party façade. Whereas Jaurès and Édouard Vaillant argued that any means, even including a general strike, must be contemplated to prevent a capitalist war, a potent German group headed by Bebel, Hugo Haase, and the Bavarian leader Georg Vollmar adopted a less categorical stance and hedged on the classic Marxist proposition that the worker knows no fatherland. In retrospect it is apparent that the pacifist idealism espoused by Jaurès was already undone. The Copenhagen congress of 1910 brought no appreciable resolution. In vain, Jaurès offered a compromise of sorts by publishing *L'armée nouvelle,* in which he attempted to reconcile nationalism with pacifism through the creation of a Swiss-style militia force to be deployed strictly for self-defense. He got nowhere, however, while the unchecked wave of demonstrations and strikes—including a major walkout of railway employees—reached a crescendo.

Germany's gunboat diplomacy in the Second Moroccan Crisis of 1911 and the ensuing tension in the Balkans brought a new urgency to Jaurès's campaign and allowed at least the appearance of greater international harmony among Socialist delegates at the Basel conference of 1912. But this soon proved to be one more rhetorical exercise, as was suggested by an embarrassing personal attack on Jaurès by the noted Sorbonne *germaniste* Charles Andler. Soon to be famed as a historian of Pangermanism, a menace recently highlighted by colonial conflicts, Andler charged that the SFIO was suffering from a fatal illusion that the SPD was equally pacifist and would, if a major crisis suddenly erupted on the Continent, cooperate in a joint strike action to prevent an armed conflict. This was to uncover the fissure that was already evident at the Stuttgart congress in 1907 and that had been thinly papered over since then. In response, Jaurès could only reiterate his shaky premise that the labor movements in both countries should and would mutually come to their senses.

For better and worse, the issue was brought to a head in 1913 by the debate over lengthening French military service from two to three years in order to meet German increases in recruitment. Better, because the SFIO and the CGT could finally agree on their opposition to a government policy; but worse, because they were thereby condemned to futility. On 7 July the bill was adopted over a strenuous objection from Jaurès by a vote of 339–223. The preceding debate, which had daily roiled republican France over a period of several months, exposed a crippling vulnerability of the Socialist position in the face of imperial Germany. The expression of antimilitarism by Jaurès and others was widely interpreted as antipatriotism and, furthermore, as a sign of weakness in opposing the Kaiserreich. One symptom of this unfavorable popular mood was a precipitous drop in membership of the CGT from seven hundred thousand in 1911 to barely three hundred thousand by 1914. Another was a noteworthy revival of the old *Action Française,* which thrived no longer on its inveterate monarchism but on a deeply felt germanophobic chauvinism.

For those who know how badly the story ends, the career of Jean Jaurès must seem quixotic, a fable of forever tilting at oratorical windmills. Yet the enthusiastic response of contemporary crowds to his extraordinary gift of speech suggests that he managed better than anyone to express a hope still held high at the time. And we should recall that his voice, in the days before radio and television, was probably heard then by more Europeans than any other in history. Nonetheless, the crisis set off in Sarajevo during the summer of 1914 was not to be contained by words alone. A hastily convened Paris gathering of French Socialists in early July adopted Jaurès's resolution to call a general strike in case of an imminent threat to the peace. But, the conspicuously unanswered question was, would German workers do the same? As the crisis approached, the Second International met on 29 July in Brussels, where Jaurès delivered the last of his moving declamations to an admiring populace. He returned to Paris at once and then, on the last day of the month, he joined his closest collaborators at the office of his newspaper, *L'Humanité,* on the slopes of Montmartre. Together they went out that evening to dine across the street at the Café Croissant, where he was assassinated at his table. Cruel to say, the most plausible epitaph in light of these events is that Jaurès was thereby spared from witnessing the complete collapse of his political ambitions. Like their German brethren, without hesitation, a large majority of French Socialists answered the call to defend their native land.

In many ways the Great War was republican France's finest hour. The loudly proclaimed *union sacrée* was never unanimous and often grudging, but the willing suspension of party differences was altogether genuine. A characteristic example was a secret meeting of executives from the private railroad companies that took place on the eve of battle. Despite repeated previous requests from the government to grant amnesty to *cheminots* suspended for their participation in the massive railway strike of 1910, the companies had heretofore refused to budge on the issue. Now, confronted with a personal plea from President Raymond Poincaré, they consented. The parliamentary vote for war credits was thus unanimous, and the Socialists entered the fray with few reservations or exceptions. Their primary objective, it is fair to conclude, was to defeat German militarism— not from motives of revenge but in order to preserve the Republic.

The political truce of the early war years was bound to unravel. It began to do so as the conflict lengthened and manifestly did so on all sides once victory was secure and the peace proclaimed. Enter

Léon Blum. Born in Paris to an Alsatian family (his father was one of the *optants* who retained French citizenship after 1870 and moved across the new Franco-German border), Blum had a nominally Jewish upbringing at home, including a bar mitzvah, though his education and orientation were thoroughly secular. He received the best of French schooling, graduating from the Lycée Henri IV, and earned a degree in law. Somewhat the dandy as a young man, he circulated in Parisian literary salons and there became acquainted with the likes of Marcel Proust, André Gide, and Paul Valéry. The influence of Blum's German-speaking parents became evident in his early writings, which notably included a long essay entitled *"Les nouvelles conversations de Goethe avec Eckermann."* In this fictitious pastiche he expressed his own youthful idealism with the voice of Goethe. As the dialogue turned to *Faust*, Blum staged a clever and scarcely disguised debate between Jean Jaurès (Faust) and Jules Guesde (Mephisto) in which the former easily outshone his satanic rival. Let it be added that at this time Blum also wrote with some admiration about Bismarck's remarkable diplomatic skill and nominated Beethoven as the noblest European of them all.

Such flirtation with German *Geist* was simultaneous with Blum's adhesion to Socialism. It has been described as a kind of religious conversion, at the age of twenty-one, that took place one evening under the chestnut trees on the Champs-Élysées. A few details are known. Importantly, Blum had been in contact with Lucien Herr—also an Alsatian—the famous librarian at the École Normale Supérieure, who introduced him to the writings of Proudhon, Marx, and especially Lassalle. He was moved by this study to declare Marx's metaphysics to be "mediocre," a line of thought that led him to adopt a revisionist stance indistinguishable from that of Jean Jaurès. The two first met personally four years later in 1897 when Jaurès was thirty-eight and Blum twenty-five, by which time the younger disciple's allegiance to his ideological mentor was already firmly established. Their last conversation occurred at the end of July 1914 when Blum accompanied Jaurès to the train station where he departed to Brussels for what proved to be his final public appearance.

Blum's prewar political activities in behalf of the SFIO were modest, while he pursued his legal career as a clerk at the Conseil d'État.

During the war he accepted a minor administrative post in a ministry headed by the old Socialist warhorse Marcel Sembat. But the wartime congresses of the Second International at Zimmerwald (near the Swiss capital of Bern) and Kienthal revealed that the *union sacrée* was rapidly disintegrating. By early 1917 there was open talk of forming a Third International, and it became clear that a movement of militants was gaining force on the French Left. Suddenly, as the war closed, central Europe was in turmoil. Major cities like Budapest, Berlin, and Hamburg became scenes of Communist uprisings. If red flags could fly from the towers of the Frauenkirche in central Munich, why not above the National Assembly in Paris? In fact, the reverberations of revolution in republican France turned out to be somewhat faint. A conservative parliament and its designated cabinets quelled a strike wave that peaked by the beginning of 1920. Nobody wanted another Paris Commune with the same consequences.

These details are essential in order to define Léon Blum's role during the interwar years. He emerged as leader of the more reticent French Socialists, those who clung to the Jaurèsian tradition of integration within the republican consensus and who therefore rejected a call to join the Third International. Famously, a definitive rupture occurred in December 1920 at the congress of Tours, where Blum departed with a small minority splinter group, deprived by the Communist majority of a united party, a large trade union movement, and a daily newspaper. These all had to be reconstituted.

Blum consequently devoted the decade of the 1920s to rebuilding his party's base, and he was extraordinarily successful. Part of his appeal was an unstinting criticism of Raymond Poincaré. Presciently, he warned Poincaré that an occupation of the Ruhr would succeed only in resuscitating extreme German nationalism and would isolate France in Europe. But his frankness earned him accusations from the Right that he was a pro-German Jew, the first salvo of an anti-Semitic bombardment that was thereafter to besiege him without cease. Undeterred, Blum supported the Dawes Plan, convinced as he was that a compromise on the reparations issue was the only path to a détente with Germany and thereby to European harmony. From this basic premise two corollaries followed. First, in foreign affairs France must award the highest priority to collaboration with Great

Britain—a sensible and yet, as it turned out, fatal assumption. Second, the Socialists must find a way to reconcile themselves with both the Radical and Communist parties in order to promote leftist solidarity. It was a delicate balance on the high wire of French politics, one that Blum performed with aplomb. Or, at least, so one must judge by the steady increase in Socialist membership that gradually tipped the weight of public opinion on the Left in Blum's favor.

He was abetted in this effort by Édouard Herriot, mayor of Lyon, the most prominent Radical politician after Clemenceau. Like Blum, Herriot opposed the rightist *bloc national* and its stated intentions to require the integral execution of the Versailles treaty, meaning the purposeful repression of a German economic recovery. This Radical-Socialist *cartel des gauches,* though still fragile in the 1920s, may be seen as a precursor of the Popular Front during the next decade. The unpredictable factor in all of this maneuvering, always a joker in France's political deck, was a Communist party (SFIC) that vibrated to the chords of the Comintern in Moscow. The SFIC's chairman Maurice Thorez was doubtless a patriot, and he was no fool, but neither was he independent.

News of the Nazi seizure of power in January 1933 thus found France in a state of confusion. The last Herriot prime ministry fell in late 1932, leaving behind it a succession of five weak coalition cabinets between then and early 1934. The contrast could not have been greater between this disarray and the single-minded fanaticism of Hitler's new regime. Accordingly, the German question now had to be reformulated once more: how could republican France possibly resist the coiled ferocity of fascism? The answer depended largely on Léon Blum.

Chapter Ten

A Strange Defeat?

A specter was haunting France. The emergence of Adolf Hitler as
the German chancellor and *Reichsführer* soon caused a case of bad
nerves in Paris. The most severe eruption in the streets occurred at
the outset of 1934. Once more all sorts of militants were active, stir-
ring up repeated demonstrations and strikes. On 6 February the
worst violence broke out in the vicinity of the National Assembly
building, where several hundred were wounded and fifteen persons
left dead on the sidewalks. Though no one could be certain quite
how seriously, the existence of the Republic was now threatened as
never before since the days of the Paris Commune.

This threat foreshadowed the main political event in France during the decade, the formation in 1936 of the Popular Front, which
made Léon Blum the Republic's first Socialist prime minister. In
truth, Blum was caught off guard by Hitler's succession and early success, believing as he did that the Nazis had already peaked in 1932.
Given his record of urging reconciliation with Weimar Germany,
Blum's first reflex was to propose a program of international disar-
mament, a transparent attempt to defang fascism before it gathered
further momentum. No one showed much interest—certainly not
Hitler—and, as it is retrospectively manifest, this policy in the early
1930s proved to be ineffectual. Blum was abruptly put on notice of

this fact by a wrenching personal experience when he was caught in a traffic jam (created by the funeral of a rightist historian, Jacques Bainville), dragged from his car on the Boulevard St.-Germain, beaten, and excoriated as a Jew. To say the least, it could no longer be self-evident that pacifism was the proper response to fascism.

Throughout the 1920s, behind Aristide Briand, republican France had relied on collective security, meaning principally its close ties with Great Britain and its alliances with smaller nations in east central Europe, the so-called Little Entente. But now it was Louis Barthou and Pierre Laval, rather than Blum, who saw that another possibility was to isolate Germany through complicity with the Soviet Union. This notion led Laval, after Barthou's untimely death by assassination, to undertake a trip to Moscow and there to confer with Stalin, even though he wished to avoid a formal military alliance with Russia. Of course, as he surely knew, this overture might also have important domestic implications, because it would soften the reluctance of French Communists to collaborate with Socialists and Radicals. A Franco-Russian nonaggression pact was signed in February 1936. That was, in some respects, the good news. The bad was that Hitler could plausibly claim that such action was a violation of existing international agreements. He thus had a perfect justification—though he would otherwise have found another if need be—for a sudden premature remilitarization of the Rhineland. A few weeks later German troops marched into Cologne. At that moment Blum, out of office and still convalescing from his wounds, was literally *hors combat,* and no other French leader could decisively react when it became clear that the British would remain noncommittal. After all, it could be argued, the Germans were only reclaiming their own territory. Yet clearly they were also taking a long stride on the route to Paris, secure in the knowledge that Anglo-French appeasement was in full swing.

These circumstances were a necessary precondition for a leftist electoral victory in the 1936 parliamentary elections and the subsequent appearance of a Popular Front. At the time this innovation was cause for a widespread celebration. But with hindsight it is easy to recognize that it was also the signal for a rapid disintegration of the republican consensus. The French nation was deeply polarized as radicals on both wings became ever more strident. On the Right the profusion of activist leagues was almost too numerous to count. Besides the *Action Française,* there were the reactionary *Croix de feu* of François de la Rocque, Taittinger's *Jeunesses patriotes,* the proto-fascist *Parti populaire français* led with a dash of Mussolini by the ex-Socialist Jacques Doriot, the so-called *Cagoule* of Eugène Deloncle, and others. On the Left radical syndicalism was meanwhile back in fashion, as militant union members saw in Léon Blum's ministry an opportunity to press their labor demands. Uncontrollably, such agitation meant a renewed wave of disruptive strikes and factory occupations.

The inglorious tale of the Popular Front has been often told. It centers invariably on two controversial topics that do not require lengthy analysis here. One was the Matignon accords concluded by an embattled Léon Blum in early June 1936, both in order to assuage labor unrest and also to realize some long-held Socialist ambitions. The main provisions included substantial wage increases (between 7 and 15 percent), a forty-hour working week, paid vacations, and some collective bargaining arrangements. Ambitiously, these were to be combined with fiscal reforms, a devaluation of the franc, and nationalization of the railroads and the armaments industry. Republican France had never witnessed such a far-reaching social and economic agenda, which was above all a laudable statement of good intentions – erratically implemented before 1940. There was simply not enough time to do everything. Besides, Blum's attention was immediately distracted by a second problematic issue, the Spanish Civil War. In essence, the agony and inaction of the French government about intervention in that struggle had already been prefigured during the earlier German remilitarization of the Rhine. The same players were acting out their practiced roles: Great Britain remained a model of neutrality; Soviet Russia was distant and aloof; Italy continued to drift toward Germany (the Rome-Berlin Axis was formally created in November 1936); and the Little Entente began to dissolve.

In all of this commotion Blum's role in France was without question pivotal, and it is therefore worthwhile to pause and consider the depth of his ambiguity, which so accurately mirrored the hesitations of republican France altogether. His initial response to the urgent news from Madrid was to offer assistance to the Spanish republicans with arms shipments; but he soon thought better of it and stopped them. His political record and his lifelong personal relations, from Jean Jaurès to Anthony Eden, inclined him to reticence. His highest priority was to preserve the peace. As a statesman Blum was thus in reality perhaps not so far removed from the pacifist wing of his party led by Paul Faure. He could not budge Great Britain, and he was fearful of provoking Hitler into further aggressive behavior (an understandable albeit misplaced concern). Blum's awkward stance recalled that of those French statesmen in the years before 1914 who had placed vain hopes in the dissuasive effect of a Triple Entente – an even less convincing pose now than then. Like many French men and women after 1918, then, Blum continued to harbor a visceral pacifism that, in his case, also contained a dark strain of pessimism. Increasingly, he became convinced that war was inevitable. At best, he could only hope to retard it while preparing republican France for the worst. This attitude helps to explain a paradox of the late 1930s when the essentially pacifist Léon Blum led a push for huge increases in the Republic's military armament. In 1937 alone, French military allocations rose over 40 percent to nearly half of the national budget. Yet time, we know, was running out.

No amount of political maneuvering could compensate for the fact that republican France was no longer a great European power. The real balance of force on the Continent was well symbolized by the May 1937 opening of the Paris international exposition at the Trocadero, where the scene was dominated by the enormously ostentatious pavillions of Nazi Germany and Soviet Russia. His nation outdistanced, his economic policy flagging, and his neutrality in the Spanish conflict under attack from both flanks, Léon Blum resigned that summer from the premiership. The Popular Front limped on for several months, but its soul was lost. Hitler obviously posed problems for which Blum—not alone—had no solution. France was shaken by the German *Anschluss* with Austria in March 1938, just as Spain was meanwhile falling to Franco. Blum was thereupon recalled to restore the Popular Front, but his second tenure as prime minister was short and sour. The Senate's refusal to grant him emergency powers hastened his resignation after only a few weeks in office. At that moment, as more than one observer correctly noted, the Third Republic seemed to be imploding.

The rest was Munich. The meeting there of the new prime minister, Édouard Daladier, with Hitler, Mussolini, and Neville Chamberlain represented an all too logical conclusion to the policy of appeasement in London and Paris during the 1930s. Even though the endemic pacificism of republican France was now clearly at risk of becoming a tragic folly, it was still popular. Having in effect capitulated to all of Hitler's demands, including the imminent dismemberment of Czechoslovakia, Daladier was nonetheless greeted like a conquering hero upon his return to Paris. The German question was thereby reduced to its starkest possible terms: the alternative between being *munichois* or not.

It follows that one curiosity of the late 1930s requires some specification. The habitual criteria for defining Left and Right on the French political spectrum no longer seemed to make any sense. Traditionally, at least since the 1870s, French leftists had been openly conciliatory toward Germany, and that continued to be the case in the 1920s (Briand was the trophy example). But the appearance of Nazism changed that by shifting Communist and Socialist opinion fiercely against Germany. Hence Blum's approving attitude toward increased French armaments was no fluke. It was in this sense not inconsistent that the last prime minister of the Third Republic was the liberal Paul Reynaud, a man now resolved to resist Nazi economic and military hegemony on the Continent – a policy, alas, adopted far too late in the day to save a desperate situation. The French Right, on the other hand, had long been characterized by ultra-patriotism and an unapologetic streak of germanophobia, traits shared even by its more moderate elements (witness Raymond Poincaré and the Ruhr in 1923). Yet the advent of German fascism caused many conservatives to alter their posture. After 1933 rightist sentiment was increasingly agitated by anti-Communism and even pacifism, thereby tilting it toward favoring rapprochement with Germany. From this reigning ideological confusion of exchanging fronts it is not difficult to deduce the further turmoil created in France by the conclusion of a Nazi-Soviet pact in the summer of 1939. Their heads spinning, the French had every reason to feel that Europe was going mad.

In the end, accordingly, there is no great problem in answering the question asked in the title of this final chapter. By 1939 the French Republic had in effect already buckled under the demographic, economic, and military weight of fascist Germany. The issue was no longer whether Nazism would dominate France but what form that domination would take. The invasion of Poland that September allowed republican politicians to make the honorable gesture of declaring war, but the French army was in poor condition to prosecute it by undertaking an offensive and chose instead to stand pat. Appropriately, it was called the Phony War, as France huddled behind the Maginot Line, fearful that the slightest movement would provoke a bombing of Paris, which might become the next Warsaw, a heap of ruins. The end approached swiftly after the German invasion commenced on 10 May. Paris was at once declared an open city while it was enveloped by a German panzer offensive that added yet another foreign word to the French language: *Blitzkrieg*. Investment of the capital began on 14 June, and on the day following, just as they had done nearly seven decades before, compact ranks of gray-clad German soldiers paraded down the Champs-Élysées. The stranger, who had for so long remained a crucial part of French public life, thus returned to Paris in triumph as the Third Republic came to its dolorous conclusion.

EPILOGUE

*A*mong historians of the Third Republic there is virtual unanimity that there was nothing inevitable about the catastrophic military defeat of France in the early summer of 1940. The French did not lack arms, or men, or courage. But they were unable to muster the organization, the efficiency, and the boldness of the formidable German *Wehrmacht*. After the lost war of 1870 republican France had been forced to restructure its entire military establishment. To a considerable extent, this effort was based on the German model in order to address deficiencies, as Marshal MacMahon put it, "that the German system alone would make it possible to avoid." Exactly like that of its neighbor, for example, the French army was divided into eighteen corps of two divisions each (rather than the arrangement, proposed by Adolphe Thiers, of twelve corps with three divisions each). It was this system, deployed behind new lines of fortification, that survived the German onslaught in the First World War. But thereafter, of necessity, Germany was the nation that needed to innovate, required as it was this time by the treaty of Versailles to start almost from scratch. And innovate it did.

The most unforgettable sentence in Marc Bloch's personal memoir and brilliant account of the French debacle in 1940 was this: "the world belongs to those who are in love with the new." For republican France, he added, this ultimate conflict was "a war of old men." The same military leaders who had heroically contested the First World War still stood faithful at their posts in the Second. Meanwhile, the protests and novel tactical suggestions of a young officer named Charles de Gaulle went unheeded by an aging *État-Major*. In love with the new? That was decidedly not the French military or political elite when massed German panzer units swept through the Ardennes and onto the plains of Champagne. Perhaps it is sufficient here to remark that republican France was tired.

It seemed altogether fitting, then, that General de Gaulle fled into exile in 1940 and that the French surrender was offered by the hero of Verdun, Marshal Pétain. For anyone who did not live in France at that moment, the enthusiasm for the Marshal's regime is difficult to fathom. For the most part, the government of Vichy was not simply tolerated but embraced. Except for those brave souls who actively joined the Resistance, this was an acceptable choice, despite the unspeakable humiliation throughout four years of watching uniformed Germans dine in the best restaurants, occupy the fanciest hotels, and sit in the most coveted boxes of the Paris Opera. "Survival is everything," as Rilke once wrote, and that is what Vichy was all about—making the best of a dreadful mess.

While Pétain, under close German surveillance, nominally presided over a divided and dispirited France, few of its citizens found reason to lament the passing of the Third Republic. True, blame for the French collapse could rest nowhere else. Yet the historical record left by republican France is not so bleak as its final episode might indicate. For most of its existence the Republic had permitted its populace to enjoy a quality of life (*"wie Gott in Frankreich"*) that was the envy of countless Europeans. Compared to the early nineteenth century, France could boast a liberal and reasonably stable democratic system of governance. Increasingly vast numbers of children attended public schools, and the literacy rate rose accordingly. An astounding quantity of goods and persons rode the rails on what was becoming one of the world's most successful networks of public transportation. Real wages were constantly rising, and hours of labor decreasing, in a workplace that was becoming both more modern and more humane. Despite nagging limitations and a lack of universal suffrage, the liberation of women was perceptibly advancing as educational barriers fell. Public health was also improving as state assistance to hospitals, clinics, and welfare agencies increased such that the post-war foundations of a comprehensive medical care system were laid.

The list could be longer. Of course we can never know what progress might have occurred under some other type of political formation that was not republican. The imponderables of counterfactual history are too slippery and tangled to handle with assurance. What is known is simply this: that after 1870 republicanism became the consensual form of the French state to which a very large majority of its citizens gladly pledged their allegiance; that its course over the seventy years that followed was deeply influenced by German proximity and presence; that its liberal consensus was in many regards beneficial to all concerned; and that its democratic tradition, once war ceased and the German occupation ended, has continued to this day in a Europe for which the close relationship of France and Germany remains fundamental.

FURTHER READING

*N*ecessarily, there is something quite arbitrary about singling out certain titles from a bibliography that might extend to several thousand titles. Yet that task is precisely what must be accomplished in order to complete this volume by providing a useful guide to other secondary works. In making the selections that follow, my apologies should be offered to all those authors of fine books that have been excluded.

Chapter One   An Unstable Past

Four consecutive volumes in the series *Nouvelle histoire de la France contemporaine,* published by the Éditions du Seuil, provide the most comprehensive and reasonably current survey available. They are by Francis Démier, *La France du XIXe siècle 1814–1914* (Paris, 2000); Jean-Jacques Becker and Serge Berstein, *Victoires et frustrations 1914–1929* (Paris, 1990); Dominique Borne and Henri Dubief, *La crise des années 30 1929–1938* (rev. ed.; Paris, 1989); and Jean-Pierre Azéma, *De Munich à la Libération 1938–1944* (rev. ed.; Paris, 2002). For anglophone readers there is no better overview than Gordon Wright, *France in Modern Times* (5th ed.; New York, 1995), one of the best textbooks ever written, always reliable and graceful. Philip Nord, *The Republican Moment. Struggles for Democracy in Nineteenth-Century France* (Cambridge, Mass. and London, 1955), is an argumentative commentary, full of interesting observations on selected topics. Of particular relevance here is the broad work of Raymond Poidevin and Jacques Bariéty, *Les relations franco-allemandes 1815–1975* (Paris, 1977), heavy on diplomatic history. Likewise, a lengthy tale of "war and insecurity" is told by J.F.V. Keiger, *France and the World since 1870* (London, 2001). For the rest one may consult, among many others, Michel Winock, *La Belle Époque. La France de 1900 à 1914* (Paris, 2002); the early straightforward account by Jacques Néré, *La Troisième République (1914–1940)* (Paris, 1965); or the more recent synthesis by Maurice Agulhon, André Nouschi, and Ralph Shor, *La France de 1914 à 1940* (2nd ed.; Paris, 2002). An interesting essay in comparative social history is by Christophe Charle, *La crise des sociétés impériales. Allemagne, France, Grande Bretagne 1900–1940* (Paris, 2001). Most of these titles are easily accessible in paperback, and all contain extensive bibliographies.

Chapter Two   AN IMPROVISED STATE

Michael Howard, *The Franco-Prussian War. The German Invasion of France, 1870–1871* (2nd ed.; New York, 1969), is lucid and concise. This basic account is augmented by Stéphane Audoin-Rouzeau, *1870. La France dans la guerre* (Paris, 1989); and by Geoffrey Wawro, *The Franco-Prussian War. The German Conquest of France in 1870–1871* (Cambridge, 2003). The episode of the Commune has been well summarized by Stewart Edwards, *The Paris Commune, 1871* (London, 1971); and by William Serman, *La Commune de Paris (1871)* (Paris, 1986). These can be supplemented by Louis M. Greenberg, *Sisters of Liberty: Marseille, Lyon, Paris and the Reaction to a Centralized State, 1866–1871* (Cambridge, Mass., 1971). The German occupation of eastern France was a subject too long neglected since the solid but now dated monographs by Hans Herzfeld, *Deutschland und das geschlagene Frankreich* (Berlin, 1924); and Karl

Linnebach, *Deutschland als Sieger im besetzten Frankreich 1871–1873* (Stuttgart, 1924). A fresh start was suggested by the symposium of Philippe Villain and Rainer Riemenschneider (eds.), *La guerre de 1870/1871 et ses conséquences* (Bonn, 1990); and the related comprehensive study by François Roth, *La guerre de 1870* (Paris, 1990). Among analyses of the republican beginnings are Guy Chapman, *The Third Republic of France: The First Phase, 1871–1894* (New York, 1962); John Rothney, *Bonapartism after Sedan* (Ithaca, 1969); J.P.T. Bury, *Gambetta and the Making of the Third Republic* (London, 1973); and Allan Mitchell, *The German Influence in France after 1870: The Formation of the French Republic* (Chapel Hill, 1979). A comparison of national symbols and celebrations after 1870 is Jakob Vogel, *Nationen im Gleichschritt. Der Kult der "Nation in Waffen" in Deutschland und Frankreich, 1871–1914* (Göttingen, 1997), a book—detailing some important dissimilarities—that is better than its misleading title.

Chapter Three   A VOLUNTARIST ETHIC

The long contest between French voluntarism and German-style obligation in social legislation received its classic definition in Henri Hatzfeld, *Du paupérisme à la sécurité sociale 1850–1940* (Paris, 1971). For the late nineteenth century this theme is amplified by Allan Mitchell, *The Divided Path. The German Influence on Social Reform in France after 1870* (Chapel Hill and London, 1991). The story is picked up thereafter by Paul V. Dutton, *Origins of the French Welfare State. The Struggle for Social Reform in France, 1914–1947* (Cambridge, 2002); and Timothy B. Smith, *Creating the Welfare State in France, 1880–1940* (Montreal, 2003). Bertrand Taithe, *Defeated Flesh. Medicine, Welfare, and Warfare in the Making of Modern France* (Manchester, 1999), is perceptively offbeat. Although relatively thin on France, a broad comparative framework is erected by Peter Baldwin, *The Politics of Social Solidarity. Class Bases of the European Welfare State 1875–1975* (Cambridge, 1990) and *Contagion and the State in Europe, 1830–1930* (Cambridge, 1999).

Chapter Four   A FLAGGING DEMOGRAPHY

Jacques Dupâquier (ed.), *Histoire de la population française, 1789–1914* (Paris, 1988), the third volume of a series, is basic. The same ground was covered more rapidly by André Armengaud, *La population française au XIXe siècle* (Paris, 1965). The role of public health in the demographic pattern is explored by Lion Murard and Patrick Zylberman, *L'hygiène dans la République. La santé publique en France, ou l'utopie contrariée 1870–1918* (Paris, 1996); and by Jacques Vallin and France Meslé, *Les causes de décès en France de 1925 à 1978* (Paris, 1988). A monographic comparative treatment is by Christian Bonah, *Instruire, guérir, servir. Formation, recherche et pratique médicales en France et en Allemagne pendant la deuxième moitié du XIXe siècle* (Strasbourg, 2000). The problem of border populations is scrutinized by Vicki Caron, *Between France and Germany: The Jews of Alsace-Lorraine, 1871–1918* (Stanford, 1988); and Hélène Sicard-Lenattier, *Les Alsaciens-Lorrains à Nancy 1870–1914* (Haroué, 2002). An important aspect of urban demography is covered by Nicholas Bullock and James Read, *The Movement for Housing Reform in Germany and France, 1840–1914* (Cambridge, 1985), which contains, however, two parallel histories rather than a single integrated comparative account.

Chapter Five   A STAGNANT ECONOMY

A starting point is the collection of thirteen essays by French economists and economic historians in Yves Breton et al. (eds.), *La longue stagnation en France. L'autre grande dépression 1873–1897* (Paris, 1997). A wider view is presented by Dominique Barjot, *L'économie française au XIXe siècle* (Paris, 1995), one of several available surveys of that topic. Richard Kuisel, *Capitalism and the State in Modern France* (Cambridge, 1981), manages to be both sweeping and penetrating. The first attempt to draft a comparison of the two nations in question was by J.H. Clapham, *The Economic Development of France and Germany, 1815–1914* (4th ed.; Cambridge, 1955), first published in 1931. This volume has been largely superseded by David S.

Landes, *The Unbound Prometheus. Technological Change and Industrial Development in Western Europe from 1750 to the Present* (Cambridge, 1972); and Alan S. Milward and S.B. Saul, *The Development of the Economies of Continental Europe 1850–1914* (Cambridge, Mass., 1977). A sound and informative comparison of national commerce is to be found in Raymond Poidevin, *Les relations économiques et financières entre la France et l'Allemagne de 1898 à 1914* (Paris, 1969). Likewise comparative, but with the focus on a salient technological innovation of the nineteenth century, is Allan Mitchell, *The Great Train Race. Railways and the Franco-German Rivalry, 1815–1914* (New York and Oxford, 2000). The French economy during the interwar years may be approached through the biographies by Pierre Miguel, *Poincaré* (Paris, 1984); and François Roth, *Raymond Poincaré* (Paris, 2000). Both the political and the economic travails of the 1920s are well analyzed by Jacques Bariéty, *Les relations franco-allemandes après la première guerre mondiale* (Paris, 1977); and by Stephen A. Schuker, *The End of French Predominance in Europe: The Financial Crisis of 1924 and the Adoption of the Dawes Plan* (Chapel Hill, 1976).

Chapter Six   A SEXIST TRADITION

Once again, the bibliographer has the *embarras du choix* in a scholarly field that is blooming. It is best to begin with Karen Offen, *Writing Women's History: International Perspectives* (Bloomington and London, 1991) and *European Feminisms, 1700–1950: A Political History* (Stanford, 2000), much stronger on France and England than Germany. But these books may be supplemented by Gisela Bock and Pat Thane (eds.), *Maternity and Gender Policies: Women and the Rise of the European Welfare States, 1880s–1950s* (London, 1991). A pioneering study, which rather tended to emphasize class more than gender, was James F. McMillan, *Housewife or Harlot: The Place of Women in French Society, 1870–1940* (London, 1981). A more feminist slant is now available in Elinor Accampo, Rachel G. Fuchs, and Mary Lynn Stewart (eds.), *Gender and the Politics of Social Reform in France, 1870–1914* (Baltimore, 1995); Mary Lynn Stewart, *For*

Health and Beauty: Physical Culture for Frenchwomen, 1880s–1930s (Baltimore, 2001), a biting appraisal of the strategies of male domination and female reactions to them; and Linda L. Clark, *The Rise of Professional Women in France: Gender and Public Administration in France since 1830* (Cambridge, 2000). Among French historians, an example of celebration is Laurence Klejman and Florence Rochefort, *L'égalité en marche: Le féminisme sous la Troisième République* (Paris, 1989); and of lamentation about the obstacles to that march, Michèle Riot-Sarcey, *Histoire du féminisme* (Paris, 2002). To date, in general, there is little to report about a Franco-German comparison, though the groundwork has been laid by Christine Fauré (ed.), *Encyclopédie politique et historique des femmes* (Paris, 1997).

Chapter Seven   AN EDUCATED ELITE

Two surveys are fundamental: Antoine Prost, *Histoire de l'enseignement en France, 1800–1967* (2nd ed.; Paris, 1977); and John E. Talbott, *The Politics of Educational Reform in France, 1918–1940* (Princeton, 1969). Katherine Auspitz, *The Radical Bourgeoisie: The Ligue de l'enseignement and the Origins of the Third Republic, 1866–1885* (Cambridge, 1982), is a brief in praise of early republican attempts to promote democracy through public education. The reluctance of the Church to adopt such reforms is examined in Allan Mitchell, *Victors and Vanquished. The German Influence on Army and Church in France after 1870* (Chapel Hill and London, 1984); and, from a Catholic standpoint, by Jean-Marie Mayeur, *La séparation de l'église et de l'état* (Paris, 1966). The slow advance in women's education is examined by Françoise Mayeur, *L'enseignement secondaire des jeunes filles sous la Troisième République* (Paris, 1977) and *L'éducation des filles en France au XIXe siècle* (Paris, 1979). Higher education is capably treated by George Weisz, *The Emergence of Modern Universities in France, 1863–1914* (Princeton, 1983). Fritz K. Ringer, *Education and Society in Modern Europe* (Bloomington and London, 1979), is valuable for its statistical comparisons of France and Germany. Artistic and intellectual contacts between the two nations are reviewed in the anthology by Michel Espagne and Michael Werner (eds.), *Trans-*

ferts. Les relations interculturelles dans l'éspace franco-allemand (XVIIIe et XIXe siècle) (Paris, 1988). As for the sprawling history of Germany's part in French intellectual endeavors in general, that subject has been expertly delineated for the period before the First World War by Claude Digeon, *La crise allemande de la pensée française (1870–1914)* (Paris, 1959). No such overarching work exists for the interwar years, but two excellent long essays shed a skeptical light on the French reception of German ideas during that era: H. Stuart Hughes, *The Obstructed Path: French Social Thought in the Years of Desperation, 1930–1960* (2nd ed.; New York, 1969); and Tony Judt, *Past Imperfect: French Intellectuals, 1944–1956* (Berkeley, 1992), which contains a harsh critique of Jean-Paul Sartre's philosophical appropriation and political use of German thought.

Chapter Eight   A XENOPHOBIC STYLE

A recent summary is provided by Laurent Dornel, *La France hostile. Socio-histoire de la xénophobie (1870–1914)* (Paris, 2004). For further study, ideally, first one would need to repeat the bibliography on French demographic trends, notably including the high number of immigrants, and then turn to the ideological debates concerning them. Zeev Sternhall, *La droite révolutionnaire, 1885–1914. Les origines françaises du fascisme* (Paris, 1978), is notorious for the argument that the rampant xenophobia of the French Right paved the way for a fascist movement, a thesis that is taken up by Robert Soucy, *French Fascism: The First Wave, 1924–1933* (New Haven, 1986). That proposition is vigorously denied in the classic statement of a Catholic scholar, René Rémond, *Les Droites en France* (4th ed.; Paris, 1982), who finds that the vitality of traditional conservatism precluded the development of a full-blown fascism in France. In turn, Rémond is taken to task by the anthology of Michel Dolby (ed.), *Le mythe de l'allergie française au fascisme* (Paris, 2003). Eugen Weber, *Action Française* (Stanford, 1962), is both balanced and minutely detailed. A notable episode is portrayed by Frederic H. Seager, *The Boulanger Affair: Political Crossroads of France, 1886–1889* (Ithaca, 1969). The real heart of the matter is expertly dissected in a single volume by Jean-

Denis Bredin, *L'Affaire* (Paris, 1983), translated into English as *The Affair. The Case of Alfred Dreyfus* (New York, 1986). Otherwise, the best short introduction to that incident is still Douglas Johnson, *France and the Dreyfus Affair* (New York, 1967). Of special interest for illuminating the shadowy background of Dreyfus's arrest and its implications is Jean-Jacques Becker, *Le Carnet B. Les pouvoirs publics et l'antimilitarisme avant la guerre de 1914* (Paris, 1973). Where all this was leading is indicated by Michael R. Maurrus and Robert O. Paxton, *Vichy France and the Jews* (New York, 1981).

Chapter Nine   A SOCIALIST REVIVAL

Still the standard narrative is Georges Lefranc, *Le mouvement social-iste sous la Troisième République (1875–1940)* (Paris, 1963). And still the best biography of French Socialism's most illustrious founder is Harvey Goldberg, *The Life of Jean Jaurès* (Madison, 1962). Incomparable is the definitive biographical study by Jean Lacouture, *Léon Blum* (rev. ed.; Paris, 1979), which now takes precedence over two praiseworthy earlier attempts: Gilbert Ziebura, *Léon Blum. Theorie und Praxis einer sozialistischen Politik* (Berlin, 1963); and Joel Colton, *Léon Blum. Humanist in Politics* (New York, 1966). For more background on the interwar years, one can peruse the essays in Jacques Bariéty et al. (eds.), *La France et l'Allemagne entre les deux guerres mondiales* (Nancy, 1987); and the German monographs by Franz Knipping, *Deutschland, Frankreich und das Ende der Locarno-Ära 1928–1931* (Munich, 1987); and Robert W. Mühle, *Frankreich und Hitler. Die französische Deutschland- und Aussenpolitik 1933–1935* (Paderborn, 1995). This story is extended by two works of Julian Jackson, *The Politics of Depression in France 1932–1936* (Cambridge, 1985) and *The Popular Front in France: Defending Democracy* (Cambridge, 1988). It is brought to a conclusion by Nathaniel Greene, *Crisis and Decline. The French Socialist Party in the Popular Front Era* (Ithaca, 1969); Guy Bourdé, *La défaite du Front Populaire* (Paris, 1977); and Anthony Adamthwaite, *France and the Coming of the Second World War, 1936–1939* (London, 1977). An essay that contains explicit comparisons of Socialism and of social welfare measures in the two countries is by Hartmut Kaelble, *Nachbarn am Rhein. Entfremdung und Annäherung der französischen und deutschen Gesellschaft seit 1880* (Munich, 1991).

Chapter Ten   A STRANGE DEFEAT?

Naturally, the first place to look is the remarkable personal testimony of Marc Bloch, *L'étrange défaite* (Paris, 1946), translated as *Strange Defeat* (London, 1949). Still useful as a record of how French conservatives shifted away from their traditional hostility to all things German is Charles A. Micaud, *The French Right and Nazi Germany, 1933–1939: A Study of Public Opinion* (New York, 1964). All analysts of the period stress both the long-term political context and the short-run military factors in evaluating France's collapse, but they tend to emphasize one or the other. Representative of the former are Jean-Baptiste Duroselle, *La décadence, 1932–1939* (Paris, 1979) and *L'abîme, 1939–1945* (Paris, 1982); and Eugen Weber, *The Hollow Years: France in the 1930s* (New York, 1994). And of the latter, Robert J. Young, *France and the Origins of the Second World War* (London, 1996); Ernest R. May, *Strange Victory. Hitler's Conquest of France* (New York, 2000); and Julian Jackson, *The Fall of France: The Nazi Invasion of 1940* (Oxford, 2003). French military reorganization is traced back by David B. Ralston, *The Army of the Republic. The Place of the Military in the Political Evolution of France 1871– 1914* (Cambridge, Mass. and London, 1967); Douglas Porch, *The March to the Marne. The French Army 1871–1914* (Cambridge, 1981); and Allan Mitchell, *Victors and Vanquished. The German Influence on Army and Church after 1870* (Chapel Hill and London, 1984). The immediate military circumstances and the *drôle de guerre* are exhaustively detailed by Jean-Louis Crémieux-Brilhac, *Les Français de l'an 40* (2 vols.; Paris, 1990). Also see Jean-Pierre Azéma, *1940, l'année terrible* (Paris, 1990). The four-year German occupation of France thereafter has an immense bibliography of its own. Here only a few of the most obvious titles can be mentioned. Pathbreaking were the works of Robert O. Paxton, *Vichy France. Old Guard and New Order, 1940–1944* (2nd ed.; New York, 1975); and

Eberhard Jäckel, *Frankreich in Hitlers Europa* (Stuttgart, 1966). More recent studies by French scholars include Jean-Pierre Azéma and François Bédarida (eds.), *La France des années noires* (2 vols.; Paris, 1993); and Philippe Burrin, *La France à l'heure allemande 1940–1944* (Paris, 1995). Business, banking, and industry are well considered by Alan S. Milward, *The New Order and the French Economy* (Oxford, 1970). H.R. Kedward, *Resistance in Vichy France* (Oxford, 1978), is still the best introduction to that controversial topic. Pascal Ory, *La France allemande (1933–1945). Paroles françaises* (2nd ed.; Paris, 1995) is an interesting albeit erratic scrapbook of relevant texts spiced with the author's commentary on them. Now the best available synthesis, a splendid work of mature scholarship, is Julian Jackson, *France: The Dark Years 1940–1944* (2nd ed.; Oxford, 2003).

INDEX

Beauvoir, Simone de, 42
Bebel, August, 63
Beethoven, Ludwig van, 66
Belfort, 10
Belgium, 56, 59
Belle Époque, 22, 26
Berlin, 14, 20, 51, 71
Bern, 67
Bernhardt, Sarah, 20
Bernstein, Eduard, 62
Bertillon, Jacques, 28
birth control, 25–26, 28, 43. *See also* demography
Bismarck, Otto von, 7, 9–11, 14–15, 19–21, 66
Blanc, Louis, 61
Blanqui, Auguste, 59, 61
Bloch, Marc, 75
bloc national, 68
Blücher, Gebhard von, 3
Blum, Léon, 62, 66–73
Bonapartism, 4–5, 7, 14–15, 41, 59
Boulanger, Georges, 10, 15–16, 59
Bourbons, 4, 14
bourgeoisie, 5, 16, 38, 63
Bremerhaven, 33
Briand, Aristide, 70, 73
Brittany, 6
Brussels, 11, 65–66
Budapest, 67
bureaucracy, 19, 44
Burgundy, 6
business. *See* private enterprise

Camus, Albert, 4
cartel des gauches, 68
census (of 1864), 26
centralism, 3, 6, 17, 53
Cette (Sète), 56

Chamberlain, Neville, 73
Chamber of Deputies, 46
Chambord, Comte de, 14
Champagne, 76
Champs-Élysées avenue, 10, 66, 74
chemicals, 22, 26, 37, 46
children, 21, 25–28, 46, 76
Christianity, 51. *See also* clericalism, Roman Catholic Church
Clemenceau, Georges, 15, 36, 52, 68
clericalism, 15, 46, 51, 52, 59
coal, 32–33, 35, 38. *See also* mining
Code de famille, 23
Cologne, 70
colonialism, vii, 34–36, 51, 64
Combes, Émile, 52
commerce, 22, 31–35, 37, 46, 76. *See also* economy, exports, imports
Commune of Paris (1871), 10–11, 13, 16, 18, 61–63, 67, 69
Communism, 59, 67–68, 70, 73
Conseil d'État, 66
conservatism, 51, 67, 73
constitution: of 1799, 2, 3; of 1815, 5; of 1830, 4; of 1875, 12
Copenhagen, 63
cotton, 33. *See also* textiles
Curie, Marie, 42
Czechoslovakia, 73

Daladier, Édouard, 73
Danton, Georges-Jacques, 4
David, Jacques Louis, 2
Dawes Plan, 37, 67
Deloncle, Eugène, 71

industry, 19, 21–22, 26, 31–35, 38, 43–45, 56, 61, 71
inflation, 35
influenza, 27
insurance, 19, 21, 23
International: Second, 65, 67; Third, 67
Italy, 56, 59, 71

Jaurès, Jean, 58, 62, 64–67, 72
Jews, 52, 55, 58, 66–67, 70

Kaiserreich, 7, 19–21, 25, 27, 33–34, 64
Kautsky, Karl, 63
Kellogg-Briand pact, 37
Kienthal conference, 67
Koblenz, 38

labor. *See* workers
laïcité, 13, 51, 52, 54
Lassalle, Ferdinand, 61, 66
Lausanne conference, 38
Laval, Pierre, 38, 70
Lavisse, Ernest, 51
League of Nations, 37
leagues, 15–16, 59, 71. *See also* politics
legislature. *See* parliament
Le Havre, 33
Lenin, 11
L'Humanité, 65
liberalism, 12, 17, 23, 53, 73, 76–77
Liebknecht, Wilhelm, 63
Ligue des patriotes, 16, 59
Lille, 56
literacy, 42, 49, 76
Little Entente, 70–71
Locarno agreement, 37

locomotives, 32, 34–35
Loi Millerand, 46
London, 73
Lorraine, 10, 16, 22, 27, 36, 53
Louis Bonaparte. *See* Napoleon III
Louis Philippe, 5
Louis XIV, 3, 5
Lourdes, 51
lycées, 42, 50, 54, 66
Lyon, 57, 68

MacMahon, Marshal Patrice de, 11, 14, 75
Madrid, 72
Maginot Line, 38, 74
Mainz, 38
Marseille, 56
Marx, Karl, 11, 59, 61–63, 66
Matignon accords, 71
Maurras, Charles, 16
medicine, 17–18, 20–21, 43, 50, 52, 77. *See also* Academy of Medicine
Mediterranean sea, 56
Méline, Jules, 58
Mercier, Auguste, 57
metallurgy, 26, 35, 38. *See also* aluminum, steel
Metz, 9
militarism, 59, 65
military, viii, 3, 6–7, 9–11, 15, 18, 36, 46, 49, 52, 56–58, 64, 70, 72–76
Millerand, Alexandre, 63
mining, 19, 33, 56. *See also* coal
Moltke, Helmuth von, 7, 11
monarchy, 1–6, 12–16, 51, 59, 64
Montmartre, 51, 65
Montpellier, 52